# No Longer Alone

# No Longer Alone

RISING ABOVE CHILDHOOD SEXUAL ABUSE

*by*

## SALLIE CULBRETH

# NAVPRESS

NavPress is the publishing ministry of The Navigators, an international Christian organization and leader in personal spiritual development. NavPress is committed to helping people grow spiritually and enjoy lives of meaning and hope through personal and group resources that are biblically rooted, culturally relevant, and highly practical.

**For a free catalog go to www.NavPress.com**
**or call 1.800.366.7788 in the United States or 1.800.839.4769 in Canada.**

© 2009 by Sallie Culbreth

All rights reserved. No part of this publication may be reproduced in any form without written permission from NavPress, P.O. Box 35001, Colorado Springs, CO 80935. www.navpress.com

NAVPRESS and the NAVPRESS logo are registered trademarks of NavPress. Absence of ® in connection with marks of NavPress or other parties does not indicate an absence of registration of those marks.

ISBN-13: 978-1-60006-392-3

Cover design by Studiogearbox
Cover image by Super Stock

Some of the anecdotal illustrations in this book are true to life and are included with the permission of the persons involved. All other illustrations are composites of real situations, and any resemblance to people living or dead is coincidental.

All Scripture quotations in this publication are taken from the *Holy Bible, New International Version*˚ (NIV˚). Copyright © 1973, 1978, 1984 by International Bible Society. Used by permission of Zondervan. All rights reserved.

### Library of Congress Cataloging-in-Publication Data

Culbreth, Sallie, 1954-
  No longer alone : rising above childhood sexual abuse / Sallie Culbreth.
    p. cm.
  ISBN 978-1-60006-392-3
  1.  Adult child sexual abuse victims--Religious life. 2.  Adult child sexual abuse victims--Pastoral counseling of.  I. Title.
  BV4596.A25C85 2009
  261.8'3273--dc22

                    2008042151

Printed in the United States of America

1 2 3 4 5 6 7 8 / 13 12 11 10 09

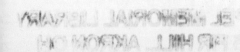

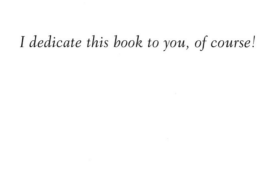

*I dedicate this book to you, of course!*

# Contents

# Acknowledgments

I thank my husband, Tim, who has been by my side through it all. To write this book took time and energy that he has graciously accommodated through his love and support; to him, for him, I am always grateful. I thank my children, Anne and Daniel, and my grandson, Kian. I have looked into their eyes and seen the face of God.

I am grateful to Derek, Dave, Cathy, Paula, Cindy, Sam, Sandy, Doris, Kristy, Mel, Patty, Dave (different one from the first!), Vickie, Roy, and Jerome. They all know what they have done for me through the years. Thank you.

I had so many people who encouraged me as this was developing that I hardly know where to begin. My parents, Jane and Frisco; my brother, Scott; Dr. Diane Langberg (author of *On the Threshold of Hope*); Dr. Vicki Tanner, therapist extraordinaire; Reverend Pam Estes, pastor of Grand Avenue United Methodist Church in Hot Springs, Arkansas; Don Simpson of NavPress, who always believed in this work and has been my advocate and friend; Greg Johnson of WordServe Literary Agency, who invested his time and talent when there was nothing in it for him; and my new friend, Jamie Chavez, my editor, who held my feet to the fire and, with the skill of a midwife, brought this book to life. I am grateful for the team at NavPress, who took a chance on me and on these ideas by publishing this book.

I am so enriched to have been on this journey with abuse survivors who taught me and helped me know what helps and what doesn't. It was their education, their honesty, and their vulnerability that has both humbled and inspired me. Finally, I am so very grateful to you for having the courage to pick this book up. I hope when you finish it you are changed and growing.

# Foreword

If you are reading this book, you have probably experienced sexual abuse as a child. You are looking for hope, understanding, and healing. Sallie has been there. And when she courageously entered the path to healing, she discovered another was there before her and with her, Someone who truly understands the suffering, the agony, the questions, and the darkness. Through this book, she desires to take you by the hand along that path and introduce you to the One who truly knows and understands.

I have listened to hundreds who have experienced childhood sexual abuse. Some have lived through one shattering instance, and others have lived through abuse that spanned decades. All have been damaged by it. They have been wounded because abuse is evil, and whenever evil touches the life of a child, damage occurs. Sometimes there is damage to the body, but always there is damage to the mind, the heart, and the soul of the child. Adults who have been victims of abuse want to understand, they want truth — about themselves and about the abuse — and they want hope. They want hope for freedom from the tentacles of abuse, hope for healing from the damage, and hope for healthy relationships with people and with God. They always want to know where God was when they were being abused.

In this book, Sallie will take you to the One who gives freedom, is truth, and will fill you with hope. He is also the One who knows and understands. His name is Jesus. The prophet Isaiah tells us that Jesus himself carried *our* griefs and our sorrows (see Isaiah 53:4). We are told he was despised, betrayed, abandoned, oppressed, crushed, and afflicted. Do those words feel familiar to you? Do they describe your experience of abuse? You see, Jesus not only experienced those things himself; He knows your experiences too. He also calls abuse evil and hates the lies it burned in your heart and mind. He wants you free. He says he came to set the prisoners free, to heal the brokenhearted, and to rebuild the ruins (see Isaiah 61:1-4).

It is my prayer that you will say yes to Sallie's invitation to come and see this God-man who weeps with you and for you. Listen and learn of him. He hates abuse, for he has told us he hates all that is evil. He is the Master Healer and can touch your heart and mind like no one else can. Yes, the road seems slow and the way long. Yes, there will be times of great pain in the healing process. A festering wound cannot be healed unless it is first opened up and then cleaned out. Such care, no matter how loving, will hurt. Without that care, death will set in. Come; learn of him. Let his suffering teach you about yours. His pain led to life, and if you follow him through your own suffering, listening to his voice speaking to you, then your pain will lead to life as well. That which was meant to be evil and soul-deadening and life-crippling will instead result in life! Walking the road with the Man of Sorrows *always* leads to resurrection!

Diane Langberg, PhD

Psychologist

# Shattered

A child's world shatters when he or she is abused. Victims' sense of goodness and safety are altered forever. They enter a personal holocaust. Everything changes. They lose themselves and will never really know who they might have been had they not known abuse. Perhaps you are one of those shattered children. You view your body, your sexuality, and your spirituality with a different set of eyes. Evil has touched you. If you give it power and permission, it will continue to victimize you.

I believe there is something unbelievably wicked and enormous in scope behind every act of abuse—*beyond* every act of abuse. The ultimate manifestation from this wicked touch is spiritual despair. Hopelessness and emptiness can become so deeply planted in a victim's heart that the shattered child can grow into a self-defeated, walled-in, hollow shell of a human. The results? Broken self. Broken relationships with people. Broken relationship with God.

Isn't it amazing that the most intimate act between people—sexual expression—is used as a weapon that can destroy the mind, body, spirit, and relationships of developing human beings? Sex was meant to be an act of celebration, covenant, and respect. It was intended to be the closest experience we have to understanding what the Scriptures refer to as "being one" (Ephesians 5:31-32). In reality, sex is sadly misused. Abuse's young victims first learn that intimacy is painful and that sexual union can create spiritual brokenness.

God knows the power of sex. It was his gift, offered for us to know and enjoy passionate expression. When the apostle Paul wanted to communicate how close our relationship with God could be, he cited the intimate relationship between marriage partners as his example (see Ephesians 5:22-33). When sex is used as a weapon to exploit rather than as a gift to give and receive, our sense of spiritual wholeness fragments into isolated, unhealthy pieces. Along with all of the other turmoil it creates, our connection with God also splinters. I am convinced this is the larger purpose of evil—to obstruct our pursuit of God and our ability to attain spiritual vitality.

This book is about reconnecting. It's a book of parallels between abuse survivors—people I have encountered over the years—and the epic, definitive story of abuse, the crucifixion of Jesus Christ. These parallels are woven together for you to consider the life of Christ, perhaps in ways you never have before. Please be aware that I have taken great liberties to re-create the experiences of Christ—his thoughts and feelings, his complex relationships, and his words. This is not intended to be an accurate historical treatment of the life of Christ or a theological study; it is a tapestry made up of stories of suffering and sorrow mutually experienced by both deity and flesh. I hope my adaptation helps you see familiar stories through fresh eyes. If you are not familiar with the life of Christ, I would encourage you to read the books of Matthew, Mark, Luke, and John in the Bible. If you are familiar with these accounts, you might be surprised by how they read once you've finished this book.

Between the lines, behind the stories of Jesus, are the complexities of life that are the human experience. God was with us for a while. That's what *Immanuel* means: "God with us." Conversations took place—with his mother, his followers, his friends, and his adversaries—that are not known to us but most certainly occurred. People talk, touch, laugh, cry, rage, act, and react. Jesus did too. Precious little is known about the myriad of details that made up all of Christ's time here. One thing is clear: Jesus was the voice of God. He clarified, explaining and reexplaining to help us understand God's extravagant love and ferocious Creator-parent passion for us.

Christ experienced no shortcuts in his journey to the Cross. He intimately understands suffering and injustice. The full impact of betrayal, pain, disappointment, and despair climaxes at that moment when Jesus—the Son of God, Immanuel—howls his heart-wrenching question, one that haunts every person who has ever suffered: "My God, my God, why have you forsaken me?" (Matthew 27:46; Mark 15:34). The anguish of that cry is not diminished by his identity. It is a legitimate question—one that even *God-with-us* needed to ask when facing such a shattered world as ours.

It is in the totality of Christ's life that the subtext of God's voice is heard. This subtext is extrapolated and embellished based on what we know about the historic, cultural, and human events of his time. Yes, words have been put in his mouth that are not precisely known and yet are not beyond the realm of possibility. Imagination beckons us to hear God's voice as he invites us to follow him beyond abuse:

*Come to me, all you who are weary and burdened, and I will give you rest. Take my yoke upon you and learn from me, for I am gentle and humble in heart, and you will find rest for your souls. For my yoke is easy and my burden is light. (Matthew 11:28-30)*

The journey toward freedom rests in identification and understanding. Although abuse brutally pummels isolation into the mind and spirit of its victims, the Cross, with equal brutality, rips open and dismantles that very isolation. If you are willing to listen, in this book you will hear the story of Christ begin with a gentle invitation to "come to me." As you join him on his journey, you will notice that the volume of his invitation grows into a resounding promise of unflinching clarity that says, "You are not alone."

# Author's Note

Many of these stories are composites of several survivors' experiences, including my own. The names and details of these stories have been modified to protect the identities of these courageous abuse survivors.

At the end of each chapter, I have included questions and prompts for self-reflection or perhaps even a group discussion. It might be helpful for you to keep a journal — where the additional space will allow you to record whatever insights occur — as you read, reflect, and respond.

Some people find great comfort from Scripture as they address the damage from abuse; others are just not there yet. As I hope you'll discover through this book, God gets it. God is not sitting up in heaven with a mallet waiting to play Whac-A-Mole with you if you aren't doing what the saint in the next pew is doing. So do what *you* have to do to nurture your heart, mind, and body. This is not an easy read. Set it down often. Build in self-care, rest, and joy as you read this.

However, I encourage you to sit with Christ throughout this book. I hope you learn to comfort each other, because you really do have so very much in common.

## The Invitation

*Come to me, all you who are weary and burdened, and I will give you rest. Take my yoke upon you and learn from me, for I am gentle and humble in heart, and you will find rest for your souls. For my yoke is easy and my burden is light.*

— Jesus (Matthew 11:28-30)

# Setup and Betrayal

*The Voice of Candy*

I loved him. I totally trusted him. I was such an idiot! So naive. I adored him, and he set me up, betrayed my trust. Oh yeah, looking back, it's easy to see how it happened. I wasn't wanted and I certainly wasn't cherished as a child—as children should be. In fact, growing up I was reminded over and over that my existence was an inconvenience. My mother and father often joked in front of me that it was too bad abortion was illegal when they found out I was on the way! Can you believe that? I wasn't wanted. I was a burden. I was in the way. I was stupid and ugly and fat. A lifetime of bitter tears can never change that. My pathetic excuse for parents is just one layer of my personal tragedy.

When I was home, I was not welcome. Even now it breaks my heart to acknowledge that. When I didn't show up, no one noticed. No one *ever* noticed me. Well, no one except my Uncle Roy, my mother's stepbrother. He lived a block away from our apartment in Chicago. Sometimes my parents would sort of forget I was outside playing and lock me out. I was just a little kid! So when they did, I'd go to Uncle Roy's. He was a few years younger than my mother and was always nice to me—at least nicer to me than my parents were.

When I started kindergarten, I spent more and more time with him. His apartment became my home away from home. We hung out together. He wasn't married. His friends were there as much as I was.

Young men. Cute men. Like Uncle Roy, they took time to listen to me, to comment on my hair or clothes or pictures that I drew at school.

By third grade, I was always at Uncle Roy's and knew all his friends really well. His friends were my friends, too. I liked it there. I preferred his apartment to that of my parents. No one at home seemed to care where I was. My parents never asked questions. I was invisible—invisible, that is, to everyone except Uncle Roy and his friends. His was the one place on earth where I mattered to someone.

One Friday night when I was in fifth grade, Uncle Roy asked me to spend the weekend at his apartment. I was eleven years old. I called my mother to ask if I could, but before I could even get the whole question out, she yelled at me for interrupting her TV show. "If he wants you, he can have you!" she said before slamming down the receiver. That kind of rejection was normal. Mother's words rolled over me, almost without wounding me that time. Almost. I turned away from the phone, from her neglect, and with a big grin announced that I could stay the whole weekend.

Pizza and movies were the agenda for that night. That's what Uncle Roy—my refuge, my best friend—told me. "Why don't you go change into your pj's," he suggested. I didn't want to miss a thing, so I hurried to change. When I came back into the living room, Uncle Roy and his friends, Jack and Sergio, were drinking beer. They offered one to me, and I jumped at the chance. "Sure!" I said, feeling so special, so included. It didn't take long until they started smoking marijuana. They offered some of that to me too. "Sure!" I said. Before long, I felt very strange, very loopy.

(Even as I tell this story, I float above myself, just like that drink and toke made me feel way back then. I have run back to that feeling again and again over the years. It has almost destroyed my life. Too many inebriated days and nights to count.)

The movies they had? Pornography. I watched with the wide-eyed innocence of a child. Uncle Roy patted his lap and told me to sit. And just as I had done for years, I climbed into his lap. Remember, I loved him and I knew he loved me, too. I would have done anything for him. Anything. The lights were out. I felt dizzy, strange. I am ashamed now to admit this, but the movie excited me. It excited Uncle Roy, too.

Before I knew what was happening, he started to take off my pajamas. I got scared and told him to stop. He didn't. Jack and Sergio moved closer to me, to us, at that point. It felt like the movie we were watching left the TV and filled the room until we all became part of it. Jack and Sergio helped him take off my pajamas and held me down. Uncle Roy took off his pants and raped me while his friends watched. Their eyes went from the TV screen to me and then back. It hurt like fire and knives inside me. When Uncle Roy was done, Jack and Sergio made me do stuff to them, but I don't want to talk about it right now.

Before the weekend was over, Uncle Roy, Jack, and Sergio had all raped me. Beer, weed, and porn were what they fed me that weekend and have been a steady part of my diet ever since. On Monday morning, Uncle Roy woke me up, fixed breakfast, and drove me to school. We all acted as if nothing had happened. The secret was sealed in my heart to fester for the next twenty years.

Jack and Sergio sat in the backseat. "You're so pretty," Uncle Roy said, touching my head, stroking my hair. "You're a real woman now," Sergio whispered, leaning over the seat. "You know, Candy," Jack said, "you're way too sexy for your age, hard to resist, you know?" He made it clear that I was the one who had tempted them. As an eleven-year-old child, I believed that if we hadn't had so much to drink or had so much weed or seen so much porn, they could have controlled themselves. Yeah, right. I was enjoying their attention yet terrified by it too. Then the car stopped in front of my elementary school. Uncle Roy kissed me — kissed me on the mouth as a boyfriend would — before I got out of the car. "I love you, Candy," he told me. No one had ever said "I love you" to me before.

Through the years since then, I've come to believe that love hurts. At the same time, to *not* be loved hurts more.

Jesus, do you know what it's like to be set up and betrayed?

## The Voice of Jesus

I knew the moment I called their names they would betray me. I did not come as an observer; I came as a participant. Relationships are what made my setup and betrayal possible. I knew they would use me, abandon me, sell me out, but I called their names anyway. I could do no less. Simon Peter, Andrew, James, John, Philip, Bartholomew, Matthew, James, Thaddaeus, Judas (the brother of James), Simon, and Judas Iscariot.

One by one, they came into my life and brought with them the passion, joy, and community I hungered for. They became my friends: my inner circle who loved me, who vowed to always stand by me, and who let power go to their heads. There they were, ready, willing, and able to enter into a relationship with me.

I had other relationships too. Before I chose the Twelve, I chose my family. I chose them before I was born, and despite all that we did to prepare them for my arrival, they were confused by me. My advent altered them and their world forever. They struggled with the events that brought about my birth, barely comprehending what was happening to them. My stepfather, Joseph, could have walked away from my mother. Any other man might have ended the engagement, might have even had her executed, but Joseph was not just any other man: He was chosen. This remarkable man remained true to my mother, assured by one of my messengers that she, too, was chosen. Together they embarked on a journey that would alter history.

My birth could not have come at a more inconvenient time for my parents. Away from home, with no familiar comforts, my mother gave birth to me. Stars and shepherds, angels and kings-with-gifts — all acknowledged my arrival. For my parents, it was overwhelming. My mother would not talk about it. She kept the entire experience sealed in her heart. With one amazing development after another, she held it in and prayed. Even when I was in her womb, I heard her prayers.

I complicated their lives. Rumors of my questionable paternity, of

Mary's morality, of Joseph's apparent unwillingness to exert his rights estranged them from their family and friends. A death sentence was put on my life almost from the beginning. My presence was perceived to be such a threat that dozens of babies were slaughtered in hopes that I would be killed too. My parents were forced to escape with me to Egypt—a foreign country—where we lived until it was safe enough to return home.

Life in our hometown went on without us. Our extended families went on. My parents' friends went on. We went on, but in ways no one would ever fully understand. You see, we were unlike any other family.

When I was still very young, we left Egypt to return to Nazareth, my parents' hometown. They would never really have a normal life again. People talked—talked about my mother, about my father, about our family, and about me. Still we settled back into our community and tried to be a normal family, even though we had to function under extraordinary circumstances.

My parents seemed to forget who I was from time to time. The year I turned twelve, we made our annual journey to Jerusalem for the Feast of the Passover. In one more year, according to our laws, I would be considered an adult. This year, however, I was recognized as a "son of the law" and began my formal religious instruction. I was trained in fasting and public worship. I also became an apprentice for my stepfather's trade of carpentry.

As always, we traveled to Jerusalem in a caravan of family and friends. This year, when I arrived at the temple, I felt the full weight of my identity and purpose. I loved Jerusalem. Loved the sights, sounds, and smells. Most of all, I loved the house of God. Because I was older, I was able to engage in deeper, lengthy discussions with our religious leaders. These conversations opened up a meaningful, rich relationship between me and my community of faith that would be ongoing for the rest of my life on earth.

I struggled to keep the perspective of my family in mind as I grew. After this particular Passover, they departed to go home, but I remained at the temple listening to the teachers and asking questions. When my parents found me three days later, I saw the panicked look on their faces. I recognized their limitations and perspectives. I gently reminded them of my identity and then excused myself from the teachers to return home. For the next few years, I remained with my parents in our parent-child relationship. My brothers and sisters grew up under my shadow. I was the brother that humiliated them because our community never fully acknowledged me as legitimate. I know it must have been difficult for them, especially when people made comments about our family. My brothers openly expressed their concerns about me. They thought I was unstable and were frequently hateful toward me.

When the time finally came for my life's work to be revealed, I was about thirty years old. My cousin John baptized me. Before the year was up, those who'd watched me grow reacted with surprising hostility toward me. A few tried to kill me. It broke my heart to know that my community—the place where I had played, grew, learned, and lived—could turn on me like that. I could almost understand strangers treating me that way, but the rejection by my own family and friends was very difficult. My lifelong relationships became the sources of wounding and pain.

Even my mother, who knew better than anyone who I was, could not overcome her own fears, her own plans, and her own ideas of who and what I should be. She pressured me to perform because she knew what I was capable of: miracles. For example, at a wedding in Cana, she asked me to salvage a catering crisis. When I challenged her agenda, she bypassed me, went to the servers, and implied that I could do something about the problem. She ignored who I was and focused on what I could do as if I were destined to be some kind of traveling magic show. Our relationship was obviously unique. Yes, I turned the water into wine, but for reasons that my mother did not understand. I did it to reveal the Father in me. With all she and I had been through together, our relationship would always remain a struggle. You see, I was not hers—she was mine.

As more and more people became followers, stronger accusations were hurled against me. It troubled my brothers and mother so much that they said I was literally out of my mind. Later, when my teachings became difficult, my followers began to drop away. My brothers noticed this and taunted my claims and my public teaching.

Perhaps most painful of all was my religious community. At first accepting, they grew to despise and blame me. Many of the same teachers who recognized my abilities when I was twelve years old were the ones who later plotted to kill me. My teachers and spiritual leaders had become my enemies. The place on earth that I loved (the temple) and those who were entrusted with the faith (the teachers and priests) brought enormous sorrow to me. I remember standing over Jerusalem shortly before my death, weeping with such angst and distress that I thought my heart would burst. My relationships with this place and these leaders crushed me. This was not just a random location on the earth; it was a site of great significance to me. These leaders were not part of an isolated, remote institution; they were the epicenter of my entire being.

And then there were my twelve disciples. Flawed. Struggling. Precious to me. I poured myself into them for more than three years, yet I knew . . . I knew they would all scatter when catastrophe struck. I knew their weaknesses and strengths better than they did. I knew Peter would deny me. I knew Thomas would doubt me. I knew John's love was strong enough to stay, but only at a distance. I knew Judas Iscariot would sell me out. I knew it from the beginning, but it still hurt when the events actually unfolded.

These men were not cruel strangers; they were my intimate friends who betrayed me. And Judas—his betrayal was the worst of all. He took what he knew, knew *of me*, and turned it against me. He knew my personal habits, my words, and my passions. He knew me, yet I wasn't enough for him. His agenda was his, not mine. Toward the end, he challenged my values and my identity. It ate at him until he brought about my demise. I warned him. I gave him an opportunity to change his mind, but he didn't.

He used our relationship to set me up. My value to him was reduced to what he could get from me: money and fleeting power. For a brief moment, he had a large army wielding swords and clubs under his tiny command, with full authority given to him by the religious leaders. Filled with smug self-importance, he led the crowd as the one in charge. Because of our relationship, he abused our intimacy that night.

I knew he was coming. I sensed it early in the day, but I stayed focused on my mission. I was in a holy place when he arrived—in a tranquil garden in solitary prayer with my heavenly Father. Suddenly, this man who knew my heart shattered my place of refuge and peace. The crowd was wild but still under his control. Then, as if time became thick with sludge, the next few moments slithered through the garden until we were face-to-face. The violence and rage were deafening.

I stood. He stood. The years of friendship and love rolled back and forth between us. I was covered in bloody beads of sweat. And then Judas Iscariot did the unthinkable: He leaned toward me, called me "Rabbi," and kissed me. His betrayal was complete. He had broken my heart.

A kiss, the sign of affection and love, instead became an act of betrayal, hurt, and death. Love hurts.

Yes, I know what it's like to be set up and betrayed.

## SELF-REFLECTION OR GROUP DISCUSSION

- Abuse does not occur in a vacuum; it occurs in a context—the context of relationship or trust, the context of neglect or loneliness. Neither Candy nor Jesus was mishandled by strangers. What their abusers knew about them was used against them. What were the relational, circumstantial, and emotional contexts of your abuse? What did your abusers know about you and your circumstances that made your setup and betrayal possible?

- Jesus was ultimately betrayed with a kiss from a trusted friend. A kiss symbolizes love, affection, and intimacy. Love, affection, and intimacy are valid needs, yet they were exploited to betray both Candy and Jesus. Because these needs are often used as part of the setup, victims can develop a love-hate relationship with their abusers. In what ways did your abuser take advantage of your needs of love, affection, and intimacy? How do you react now when you have those needs?

- How would you have tried to comfort Candy when she was a girl? How would you comfort her now?

- What would you like to say to Jesus about his experiences with setup and betrayal?

# Filled with Dread

## The Voice of Jeremy

By the time the last bell rang for school to let out each Friday, I was already a wreck. The ring signaled the beginning of another three-day marathon of abuse. Other kids from my class seemed excited about the weekend, but my movements became slower and slower. My breathing got shallow. I was listless, in a disconnected, dreamlike state. And at the same time, I was hypervigilant. Inside I was going crazy. The ringing in my ears deafened me, and I was imprisoned in my aloneness. No protection. Nowhere to run. I was on my way toward another weekend from hell—on my way back to the dilapidated slum apartment in Brooklyn that I called home.

I was the youngest of three boys. None of us had the same daddy. Mama worked two minimum-wage jobs to provide for our family. My father, the last of her men, had abandoned us long ago. We were on our own during the weekends because of this.

It's difficult to remember exactly when the abuse started, but it was somewhere around age five. I seem to remember a connection between starting school and those weekends of horror, but, honestly, it's something I've worked hard to forget. Still, there are things I can't forget—things that still haunt me today, even as a grown man. That terrible sense of dread. I suppose it serves me well in my work—I'm a detective for the NYPD—but my constant expectation of horror has devastated my inner life and my ability to really be a free man.

My brother William was eight years older than I, and Edgar, my other brother, was seven years older. They formed a gang of terror that lasted into my teenage years, when I finally grew big enough to protect myself. But even then, the routines were set in stone. Friday night the threats began. William and Edgar would circle me, poking at me, tickling me, thumping my head, and hitting me with pillows. Each poke, tickle, thump, and wallop with the pillow was accompanied by, "Hey, Jeremy, Sunday's comin'! Get ready! Sunday's comin'!" They were in charge of me, a job given to them by my mother. They were supposed to feed me and watch out for me, but I paid an excruciating price, walking their death march in order to survive.

William prepared dinner on Friday night, but Edgar made me beg on my hands and knees if I was going to eat. My performance had to be pretty dramatic in order to get food, and sometimes they would add other requirements, like licking their feet or eating off the floor like a dog. It went like this throughout the whole weekend. By Monday, I was usually starving when I got to school, always thankful for the breakfast and lunch programs I got because we were so poor.

On Saturday, their torment escalated because they were sick of taking care of me. I'm sure they just wanted to hang out with their friends and be normal teenagers, but our family's circumstances forced all of us to grow up faster than we should have. I became the scapegoat for this reality, at least with my brothers. They would barricade me in the closet or hang me out our sixth-floor-apartment window by my feet. Their pokes and tickles turned to slaps and punches. Mama's schedule was pretty regular, so they knew just how long they had and how much they could do to me without causing a visible wound or a terrible mess in the apartment. I knew I could never tell her what was going on. If I had, even if she'd believed me, there was nothing she could have done to protect me. She had to work or we'd be homeless. Eventually, she would have to leave for work, and then I'd pay for telling.

Every Sunday we went to church. Rain or shine, snow or heat wave, we went to church. Mama was a devout Christian woman, and her work schedule accommodated church attendance. Church, for me, was the final prelude to the ultimate violation of the weekend.

We attended a church known for its enthusiastic worship—lots of singin' and dancin', preachin' and prayin', as they say. Our services would last from early Sunday morning until mid-afternoon. Mama left as soon as church ended to get to her job. My brothers and I walked home. They would flank me on both sides, lock our elbows, and escort me home. By the time we walked the eight blocks, I was nauseous and nervous. Every muscle in my body twitched. I was both freezing and sweating at the same time. We walked up our six flights of stairs—past screaming babies, fighting couples, and the stench of pee—to our apartment. William opened the door; Edgar dragged me to the bathroom and threw me in, closing the door behind me. I heard them laughing in the kitchen as they ate. I frantically dug through the laundry hamper and began putting on as many pairs of underwear and pants as I could find. I did this every Sunday afternoon, and every Sunday afternoon it was useless to try to protect myself.

For hours, I crouched in the tub, hoping they would forget I was there, but they never did. They stood outside the door, tapping. This was the beginning of the end, when the tapping started. More than once, I thought I should just open the bathroom window and jump, but I never did. Even now, I sometimes feel that same urge to die, especially on Sunday afternoons. Their tapping progressed to jiggling the doorknob—never opening it, just jiggling it. I could see it turning back and forth slightly, but my brothers meant to scare me with only the sound. They accomplished their goal. I was terrified. Soon the sun went down and the bathroom went dark. I pretended to fall asleep—maybe then they would leave me alone—but nothing ever changed. The apartment went silent. The pounding of my heart and the ringing in my ears shook my entire body.

Then I heard them. Footsteps coming back down the hall. I heard the doorknob turn. The dread got to me long before they did. For several hours after that, William and Edgar would sexually abuse and then beat me. My brothers laughed as each layer of clothes was peeled from my small body, as if those layers could have somehow protected me from this hellish existence of mine. Once they were finished, once there was nothing left of them or me, they turned an ice cold shower on me, a broken little boy, and left the bathroom.

For three days each week, I was in the grave of violence, torture, and abuse. Throughout my childhood, I lived in dread of what the weekends brought. I begged God to make my abusers go away, to leave me alone. I prayed, as Jesus did, that this cup would pass, but it didn't. Even now, as a grown man, Friday ties me up in knots of anxiety and fear, Sunday almost levels me like a bomb blast, and Monday continues to be the greatest day of the week.

Jesus, do you know what it's like to be filled with dread?

## The Voice of Jesus

The years had warned me. These were coldhearted, merciless people. They were behind the arrest and murder of my cousin John. They entrapped a woman to commit adultery and then orchestrated her circumstances in an effort to entrap me. They systematically played mind games with me, persistently undermining my teachings and my growing popularity. They stalked me. They infiltrated my followers. They exploited their influence and spread their poison in order to sabotage me. But I knew them—knew what they were capable of.

They tried every trick in the book to annihilate me, to call into question my message and my integrity. First I was called a glutton and a drunk. Then I was accused of blasphemy because I healed a man and ate wheat that we picked from a field on the Sabbath. I was labeled an anarchist when I cleared the temple of exploitive merchants and was called a defiler when I spoke to those outside of our faith and race. Doubts were raised about my handling of finances and taxes; I thought that both Rome and my own people might try to convict me, but I pointed out whose face was on the coin and that silenced them for a moment. They judged me as a sinner when I befriended men and women who did not meet their standards of holiness. They never got me though, never conquered me.

They were so common, so predictable, so mean. Even though they were creatively cruel and dangerous, I always won, always answered correctly, always left them confused and exposed. But they didn't play fair—never had and probably never would. As I said, the years had warned me of what they were capable of. But all of their past failures to interrupt me, to silence me, to end my work would come to a boil. I had seen the warning signs. Soon they would have me right where they wanted me.

Judas left our last supper quickly. Dread crept into my heart. Even as we were singing our hymns before the meal ended, my stomach began to turn and muscles began to tense. I knew what was coming and I knew it would be bad. I felt so alone, so sad. I desperately needed my friends to be with me, to pray with me, but they were frail. I knew that, but it didn't diminish my need. We went to the Garden of Gethsemane and I moved up the hill to pray. I was suddenly so overwhelmed with what was at hand—overwhelmed to the point that I began to convulse and sob.

As I fell to the ground, my body racked with anguish and sorrow. I began to pack myself in layers and layers of desperate prayers. In vain, I tried to pull God's love and peace up around my heart like a warm blanket. I urgently sought to wrap his purity and sacredness around my mind. Could I possibly encase my fragile flesh in something noble and safe? Strong and comforting? As I said, I knew what was coming. I hoped, *begged* for a way out, but I was trapped. They were already on their way.

Besieged by the events about to unfold, my body reacted with such swift force that the capillaries burst on the surface of my skin. There in the garden, with bloody drops of trepidation falling from my face, I saw the torches, heard the mob, and felt the evil. Those sounds, those sights, those people who were bent on hurting me, all of it filled me with dread so real I could smell it, taste it. Even knowing the beginning from the end, the malevolent starkness of torture paralyzed me. It was almost Friday. The nightmare was waiting to be experienced. My blood-wrenching anxiety was very real. Monday seemed to be an eternity away. I prayed that somehow this cup would pass, but it would not.

Yes, I know what it's like to be filled with dread.

## SELF-REFLECTION OR GROUP DISCUSSION

- Sometimes dread involves more than just the experiences of abuse; it can also involve the dread of discovery or the dread of consequences. As you reflect on your abuse, what was it that you dreaded?

- Abuse often has a routine to it—a ritual that the abuser uses before the abuse begins. The routine contributes greatly to the sense of dread. Both Jeremy and Jesus experienced physical and emotional reactions to dread. What were your physical and emotional reactions to dread? When you experience dread now, how do you feel physically and emotionally?

- Why do you think Jesus allowed himself to experience dread? What does that have to do with your experiences? How can this knowledge help you?

# Abandonment

## The Voice of Steve

My father was a politically powerful man, very influential and very wealthy. He and my mother had a strained relationship, and they both strayed into the beds of other people quite often. My father never treated me as he did my siblings. I never knew why, but I suspect he thought I wasn't his. There was no proof of that as far as I know, but that's how it always felt to me.

I grew up under his harsh, critical eye. There wasn't much I could do right, but that never stopped me from trying. Regardless of my efforts, it was never enough. My mother did little to protect me from his tirades, whether verbal or physical. I think she was as terrified of him as I was. I slipped further and further behind in school, drowning in one unsuccessful grade after another. I was so overwhelmed by my father's expectations of me that I pretty much stopped trying.

I colored outside the lines. The dog ate my homework. Teacher, he hit me first. I stayed in the corner. My lunch tray landed on the floor by accident. No one bothered me on the playground. Just wait 'til I tell your father! Elementary school was a nightmare. Coming home each day was a bigger one.

Our home was always filled with important people—people of affluence and clout who worked closely with my father on political campaigns or union issues. It was funny to me that he seemed a bit intimidated or afraid of many of these men. I got secret satisfaction from watching him sweat when they were at our house. He was worried about my mother's cooking, how clean the house was, how well behaved we kids were.

He was nervous that these powerful people might not like his ideas or decisions, so he overexplained everything to the point that they always became annoyed. For reasons still very unclear to me, my father owed something to these powerful political people in our small, corrupt industrial town in Indiana. Their sticks seemed so much bigger than his—that is, until they left. Then his stick became the bigger one, bigger than ours, and was often used against us in vicious ways. The power struggle went down the food chain from my mother to my brothers and sisters and then to me. Home was a brutal place, not a sanctuary of love and security by any stretch of the imagination.

One of my father's powerful friends was a man named Mr. Winston. He was a local politician who had strong union ties and owned enormous amounts of property. He pretty much served on every board or committee in town. People groveled before him, acquiesced to him, and never, ever crossed him. He demanded absolute loyalty and got it. So far-reaching was his influence that it seemed he always knew if someone had so much as mentioned his name behind his back.

Mr. Winston was a scary man, yet he liked me. My father couldn't understand it, but in his eyes it seemed to be the one thing I had going for me. When I was around the age of eight, with the full support of my parents, Mr. Winston began to take me under his wing. He took me fishing, to ball games, and to restaurants. He complimented me often in front of my parents, and if my father dared to say anything negative to me, Mr. Winston swiftly corrected him. I think at one point my father was actually jealous of me, but he never verbalized that.

Soon there were overnight visits to Mr. Winston's mansion when his wife went to visit her family out of town. It was there that Mr. Winston gave me my first drink, showed me my first glimpse of pornography, and slept with me for the first time. In the beginning, that's all it was;

we slept in the same bed. Over time, however, the sleeping turned to fondling and then to sex. I was afraid. I felt as though what was going on was very wrong, but I knew there wasn't much I could do about it. After all, I was only a kid. Mr. Winston always bought me something new or gave me a special treat, like taking me to a movie or going hunting. He carefully maneuvered me into guilt with his gifts, attention, and special treatment in order to ensure my silence. The thing most empowering for me was how he desired me and intimidated my father. That false sense of empowerment kept me compliant and silent.

Yes, there were parts of what happened that gave me pleasure. For that I still cannot forgive myself. Still, I did not like what Mr. Winston was doing to me. The sexual abuse got weirder and weirder, sometimes even painful, but I couldn't stop it. My father's fear of him and the mountain of gifts and special treatment, which proved he was a "good man," trapped me. The escalating sexual abuse became unbearable to me, and I finally told my father, naively expecting him to protect me. Where I got the idea he would do that is still beyond me. I guess it was just a child's hope that proved completely unfounded.

When I told my father, he went ballistic, but not at Mr. Winston — he was mad at me! He called my mother in and began to yell about what a filthy pervert I was. He screamed at her, he screamed at me, and then they both screamed at me. It was more of a nightmare than Mr. Winston's exploitation of me.

I was sent to my room, where I could hear the muffled shouting between my parents. It continued for about an hour. I curled up in a ball in the corner of my room. Soon my father exploded through the door and looked at me cowering in the corner. "Pathetic liar!" he roared. "If you ever tell anyone about Mr. Winston and your ridiculous made-up stories, something very, very bad will happen! Do you understand me?" It was hard to imagine anything worse than the reality of my life, but I believed that my father had the capability of making it worse.

Then my parents stopped talking to me and cut me off from all family functions. I was no longer allowed to eat with my family. I was forced to stay in my room for hours at a time in a fetal ball. The hardwood floors in our house creaked at the slightest pressure. My father told me that if I moved from that position and he heard the floors creak, he would beat me. Sometimes my knees and back would ache with stiffness from holding that position so long. Sometimes I would need to use the bathroom. Then the floor would creak as I moved and, true to his word, he'd fulfill his promise.

Because I told about Mr. Winston, I was excluded from holidays. My father would wake me on Christmas morning and scream at me the entire way down the stairs, where I was told to sit and watch as my siblings opened their Christmas gifts. My siblings and my mother never even looked at me as they opened their presents. There was none for me because I told on Mr. Winston. Filthy, perverted liars do not deserve Christmas presents or birthday presents or family meals or words.

Mr. Winston still came over for a few more years. I was still sent away with him to his house or on trips. Eventually, as I began to mature, Mr. Winston found a younger boy to groom and stopped paying attention to me. I was relieved, but I was also devastated because I was no longer special to anyone. My father was furious—furious at me, not Mr. Winston! I found out, you see, that Mr. Winston could have done bad things to my father if this had ever been reported. Once Mr. Winston stopped sexually abusing me, my father chased after him like a dog in heat. All the while, I was reminded again and again that I was no son of his and that I ruined the only chance I ever had. Do you realize that I "blew it" by no longer being a victim? My sexual abuse was not the only thing obscene about my childhood!

I was ten years old the last time anyone even pretended to care about me. My family discarded me then. Eventually, so did Mr. Winston. Left alone, I was abandoned by those who should have loved and protected me. Being alone hurts, but it's easier to be alone, I guess.

Jesus, do you know what it's like to be abandoned?

## The Voice of Jesus

This was to be our last supper together. Judas left us abruptly after I told him to do what he was going to do quickly. Our Passover meal was almost over, yet there was still so much I needed to explain to my friends. I wanted them to be prepared. I carefully and firmly laid out the unfolding events, but they refused to embrace my words. Peter, emboldened by a warm meal and our intimate gathering, declared in his usual brash way that nothing was going to happen to me as long as he was around. Along with the others, he affirmed that he'd always be there for me. I gently explained that he wouldn't. Of course, he saw that as a challenge and met it with his bold assertion of undying loyalty. I responded to that with a foretelling of what would soon become a bitter reality: He was going to abandon me. The room chorused with promises of faithfulness and fidelity.

My small gathering of followers had good intentions that night, but soon enough they would find out what they were really made of. I knew the time was closing in on me. I urgently needed strength from my heavenly Father before the closing events of my time on earth began, so after dinner we walked to the Mount of Olives. This was a place where we regularly met. Through the years, its beauty and serenity brought comfort to me, and tonight I needed that more than anything. As we walked, everyone was talking. Some were singing. I was silent. Even though I tried to prepare them for what would soon take place, they simply did not grasp it. I think they assumed this was still some far-off, distant threat and not something that would happen in the impending moments and days ahead. I knew better.

I loved these beautiful, flawed, resilient people. After all our years together, they knew me well. My habits, my temperament, my teaching, my passion, my practices—all were familiar to them by now. I had become vulnerable with them. My heart became open for them to peer into, where they could get a glimpse of my Father. Sometimes they understood, but most of the time they didn't. They tried, they truly tried, yet I knew that the most critical lessons for them were about to come.

My little band, my family of choice, all grew quiet as we neared the garden. With each step, I could feel the air become thick, heavy with a dark sadness that was palpable. I needed them to stand by me. The intensity of that need almost took me by surprise, especially because Father and I had been planning this for so long. There it was, however — my need for them at this hour. It was a simple thing that I asked of them: "Sit and pray while I go a small distance to do the same. Keep me company, please."

I asked my closest companions — Peter, James, and John — to go further on with me, which they did. In my hour of need, I turned to my three friends for support, but instead I saw shock and even terror on their faces. They had never seen me like this before. I pled with them to stay with me, to pray with me, to be there for me. Their eyes grew wide as I fell to the ground to pray, lost in the realm of my Father for a time, asking him if there were any way to escape what was about to happen. There wasn't.

I felt a bit calmer after prayer, so I rose to check on my frail friends. They were asleep! It didn't enrage me as much as it saddened me. All I asked of them was to remain and pray with me. They did neither. My concerns were for not only what awaited me but also what awaited them if they did not draw upon my Father's strength while there was still time to do so. I knew that if they failed me over the next few hours, their sorrow would be almost as unbearable as mine. In my need for support and companionship, their sleeping left me feeling starkly alone and abandoned.

I left again to pray. Again my three friends fell asleep, and again I awoke them. They cowered in shame. One last time I prayed, one last time they slept, and then the moment the ancient texts foretold arrived. The garden was filled with an angry mob led by Judas. Lies. Rage. Accusations. Confusion. It was bizarre. Surreal. Everything slowed down. Every action, word, and sound seemed to be suspended in time. I was arrested.

My followers panicked as the horde of priests, temple guards, elders, and servants descended on me. One of the servants wielding a sword came toward me, but Peter—blinded by fear—grabbed it and began slashing him. He actually chopped off the servant's ear. I couldn't believe it. For three years, I'd taught them about peace and nonviolence, and here we were, confronting the corruption of religion and civil society with an act of equaled violence. "Stop! Stop!" I screamed. For a brief moment, the whole circus paused. I looked in disbelief at my followers and told them to end such behavior immediately. The violence Peter exhibited in that moment shocked me. In many ways, this was the moment when he'd first abandoned me. He turned his back on all that I stood for and taught. I took in a deep breath, closed my eyes, and healed Malchus's ear. Both the cutting and the healing silenced the crowd, and then insanity seized control again. I was swept away to face my accusers.

My little group fell apart. Lies. Distortion. Perversion. If I could have watched from a distance, it would have been the most outrageous scene imaginable, but I wasn't watching from a distance. I was there. It was real. I stared evil in the face, and it stared back at me.

My followers kept their distance from that point on. Only a few dared to move in, although none of them was really sure about what to do. After all, they were just about as powerless as I was. It was cold as the night progressed. I was the object of unbelievable hatred, so vicious that it disoriented me. A courtyard fire was lit to warm some of the mob. Peter actually came and sat down with them. Whispers turned to words spoken out loud—words that pressed Peter to admit that he knew me. I'd told him this would happen, told him it would happen three times this night, but he did not believe me. Put more appropriately, he did not believe himself to be capable of denying his relationship with me, but he was.

Peter said he didn't know me once. He got up and walked away, but then someone else questioned him. This time he swore he didn't know me with the foulest language I had heard him use since the very first time we'd met. Then, he was a bawdy fisherman with a temper and a mouth to match it. That was a man I hadn't seen surface in a long, long time—that is until now. One last time he was pressured, and one last time he claimed to have no idea who I was. Then a rooster crowed on cue.

I was so tired, so cold, so sad, so afraid. His denial crushed my heart. I looked up. Our eyes locked and all of that sorrow poured out between us. He ran away. My boisterous, brash friend ran away. I don't know if it was his violent weeping or mine that I heard more loudly. The harsh reality for me was that this man, my friend, my trusted friend, was more concerned about his own well-being than mine. He was terrified of those conducting the inquisition and abandoned me because of it. I was alone—truly alone among men. Alone hurts.

Yes, I know what it's like to be abandoned.

## SELF-REFLECTION OR GROUP DISCUSSION

- Both Steve and Jesus experienced physical and emotional reactions to abandonment. Both needed to depend on others for loyalty and comfort. Describe the people you needed to depend on for loyalty and comfort. How did they fail you?

- Both Steve and Jesus had intimate relationships with people who kept their distance when the abuse began. These people experienced their own terror and weakness. They were so concerned for their own safety that they turned away. What did those passive people in your life have to be afraid of? What were their weaknesses? Describe how those you were close to kept their distance when the abuse took place.

- Could Jesus' followers have done anything to prevent what was happening to him? Could those who were passive and close to you have done anything to prevent what happened to you?

- Why do you think Jesus allowed himself to experience abandonment? What would you like to say to him about this?

# Exposure and Humiliation

### The Voice of Liz

Even now, I shudder with shame as I tell about this. Then I was just a kid—a lonely, confused teenage girl looking for some fun. Yep, I was a good little church girl. We went to church every time the door opened. My Christian parents were very strict and so overprotective that I could hardly breathe. I resented them for it but never really voiced my feelings for fear of invoking an end-times apocalyptic conflict that had the potential to last for days, followed by long prayer meetings. Because prayer cured everything, you know. So it was just easier to sneak out or make up elaborate stories that they readily believed. I was the model daughter, a good girl who loved God with all her heart. That's what they believed, anyway. As long as they did, I remained undetected. Like a lot of my friends, I was doing stuff I knew I shouldn't do. Drinking. Drugs. Partying. Sneaking out at night. I knew better, but I did it anyway.

Jesus seemed to be the cure-all—the magic bullet when you really messed things up. Week after week, we heard "testimonies" in church from former drug addicts and alcoholics who had lost everything but then miraculously found their way back from the edge. There was an endless parade of reprobates who supposedly had stepped over the line, only to become good enough now to stand behind a pulpit. So how bad could it be?

I guess I thought I had some kind of super safety net if I ever needed one. Jesus had been crammed down my throat my whole life, and, frankly, I was sick of the rules, the dress, the hysteria. The expectations were high for me. I was to go through life with no great stories of depravity, no tales of corruption. There would be hell to pay if I didn't walk the narrow path—literally hell to pay, as in *I would go to hell*. Every word I spoke, every thought and action, had eternal weight to it. The pressure was unbearable. The somber life of my family filled me with bitter resentment. After all, the straight and narrow never got top billing at church. It didn't sell books or movies, and it certainly didn't sell me.

So by the time I was fourteen, I had pretty much established myself in the world of the fringe kids—kids who were from homes very different from mine. Violence, abuse, addicted parents, adults who acted like children, children with no choice but to be adults—these were the things my friends dealt with every day. I lived in a home where my parents had been happily married forever, where we had meals together, where we were expected to do something worthwhile with our lives, and where I was loved, supported, and cherished. My world and that of my friends couldn't have been further apart, yet it was to theirs that I gravitated.

Thrown into this mix was the lofty goal of staying a virgin until my wedding night. True Love Waits, an abstinence-only program, came to my church and, like all the other kids in my youth group, I put the ring on my finger and vowed I would remain pure until my wedding night. Then I would lovingly take this same ring from my finger and give it to my husband before we consummated our love, letting him know I had saved myself for him. Yep, the ring and my body would be his. These were the values of my upbringing, and I guess at some level they rattled around in my value system, too, but didn't create enough noise to make a real difference in my choices.

Like so many other times, one night I made up an elaborate story about spending the night with a friend from church. My mother trusted me completely, and because she did, she never verified my plans. She dropped me off at my friend's house. I kissed her cheek to say good-bye, and she told me to have a good time—which I intended to do, as soon as she was out of sight.

My friends—my dark, brooding, angry friends—were waiting for me around the corner. I changed clothes as fast as I could, stuffed them into my bag, and went from Sunday school poster child to "ho." I proudly wore the uniform of my angst tribe. I was still so naive that I had no idea what or who I truly needed to be afraid of. That lesson was coming up very quickly.

We went to the part of town where kids congregate at night to do stuff we are not supposed to do. The cops constantly tried to run us off, but like a flock of birds, we would settle back down to whatever we were doing as soon as they were out of sight. The adrenaline rush was energizing to me. Yep, I was building a testimony for sure. I could so picture myself standing at the pulpit one of these days, telling stories that would make the sisters gasp and the brothers shake their heads.

That night, I had a substantial bag of marijuana in my purse. I figured I could sell some of it for a little extra money. A car full of "white hats"—preppy boys in their late teens with too much money and ego—pulled up next to my band of misfits. They whistled and made comments about how hot I looked, so I went over to talk to them. Keep in mind that I was only fourteen. As the flirting escalated, I showed them my bag of weed and told them they could buy some if they wanted to. Of course, they responded with great enthusiasm and told me to jump in so we could seal the deal away from the crowd. I got in and away we went. There were four of them.

We pulled up behind some kind of abandoned office park. One of the white hats had a key and said that it had been his old man's office but he'd just moved to a new one. He looked at me and told me we could go inside and he would give me money for the weed. I felt a bit nervous but didn't want to appear immature or inexperienced, so I got out of the car as if I had done this sort of thing a hundred times before. I hadn't.

We all walked into the office. The white hats turned on a side room light so it was dim in there but bright enough to see. Then the four of them circled me like hungry wolves, and I knew I was in trouble. They stripped me naked and then gang-raped me, laughing the entire time. They were rough and coarse and callous. They called me horrible names and kept telling me that I could thank them for making me a woman. All the while, they laughed at my immature body and foolish trust. One of them even urinated on me as I lay there. After it was all over, they took my clothes and bag, threw them into the back parking lot, and took off without me. I was a joke to them. They roared with laughter as they drove away. They left me stripped, urine-soaked, raped, and naked. To top it all off, they took my bag of marijuana, too.

I was completely exposed—I had nothing to cover myself with and was bleeding badly. That was nothing compared to the bleeding in my heart and the terror in my mind, though. I crouched down as low as possible, trying to cover my body, and bolted from the office door, looking frantically for my clothes and bag. Passing cars sent me scurrying for cover, but there was none. I was in a parking lot, naked, bleeding, and completely exposed.

I grabbed what I could and dashed behind a garbage dumpster to get dressed. I was shaking so badly I could hardly get anything on, but another set of car lights once again energized me to get covered. I got a few things on but couldn't find everything I'd worn there. They must have taken some of my clothes or flung them too far for me to find. In my bag were my Sunday school poster child clothes, so that's what I put back on.

For the next few hours, I walked in a confused daze trying to find someone who could get me home. I made it back to one of my friend's apartments, who let me take a shower and clean myself up. This brutal rape was never reported, the enormous wound in my life never tended to. I could never tell those who truly loved me, who could have helped me through it, because my double life and shame would be exposed, like my body was with the white hat rapists. For years, I blamed me, not them. I know now that my foolish adolescent choices put me in a dangerous situation, but their incomprehensible cruelty and perversion — well, that was on them. This crime was theirs and theirs alone.

Exposure of my body to these barbarians was humiliating. If anyone else knew about what happened, the exposure of my shame would have been even more humiliating. At least that's what I believed for many years.

Jesus, do you know what it's like to be exposed and humiliated?

## The Voice of Jesus

I was exhausted. I had been up all night when the next stage of my nightmare began. It was early morning. Pilate didn't do the right thing. He didn't stand up to Caiaphas or the chief priests and elders. I was expendable, insignificant. He actually washed his hands in front of everyone as if that absolved him of this one atrocity, when there were so many other horrors to his credit. The governor's soldiers were summoned to begin their monstrous task.

I was to be flogged. The soldiers took me into the palace called the Praetorium for the public beating. The instrument of torture was a wicked invention called a flagrum. It was a large whip that had three smaller whips attached. These smaller whips were encrusted with shards of bone and metal; when they hit my skin, they wrapped around me like tentacles and pulled back large sheets of flesh with each blow. It would have been illegal to use this on me if I had been a Roman citizen, but I was not. I was an object of amusement for this group of professional executioners.

It wasn't enough that those charged with my flogging were already leveling the crudest, most vulgar insults my way. They even summoned the rest of the company to come watch. I found myself in this place of cold stone and dust. Every word echoed as it was hurled my way. My fatigue, hunger, and dehydration caused me to become dizzy and nauseous, but those were the least of my problems.

Before I knew what was happening, the soldiers ripped my clothes off my body. I was left standing naked in the center of the vilest, most hate-filled circle imaginable. My hands were bound so I could not cover myself. I was jabbed, grabbed, and dragged through the mob of soldiers. The noise was deafening. They lashed my wrists to the whipping post, and then the flagrum wielded its destruction on my naked flesh. With each blow, the whole company cheered, snarling slanderous insults at me as one more shred of skin was peeled from my body. The whips wrapped around to my chest, around my thighs, even around my genitals, leaving nothing but mutilated flesh. Thirty-six, thirty-seven, thirty-eight, thirty-nine! Was it over? Far from it.

They cut me down and put a robe over my naked, bleeding body. One of the more sadistic soldiers made a crown out of enormous thorns that penetrated not only my scalp but also the soft, thin bone of my skull. I could hear the bone giving way to the massive thorns. Like an animal, I was led around the room. Every inch of my body was exposed except for my back, where the robe was stiffening as my blood coagulated to it. Each taunting man spat on me with such malice as I passed that my heart became as shredded as my flesh. Some ripped out my beard, some punched, and some kicked. The brutality was mind-numbing.

I was not sure if this scene would ever end, but it finally did when they ripped off the robe. As the robe was pulled away, it re-tore my sliced skin, and the bleeding began again. Now it was time for the parade. The horizontal wooden post that would become part one of my cross was strapped to my wrists. It probably weighed over forty pounds and I was incredibly weak by this time. I was forced to walk through the streets of my city, my Jerusalem, bleeding, naked, and brokenhearted.

The people who had greeted me like royalty only a few days earlier now jeered at me as if I were the lowest form of vermin on the planet. To be the object of so much hatred shattered my heart long before it killed my body. The echo of words, as mean and brutal as the beating, pierced my mind and spirit.

Once I was nailed to the cross, it was raised and dropped into place. And when I thought nothing more could be taken from me, another appalling insult took place. The clothes they'd stripped me of were laid out before me, and the soldiers gambled for my clothes. I hung on that cross, dying and exposed, my tattered clothes going to my executioners, with the angry mob cheering them on. In that mayhem, there were not only innocent children but also my mother and my followers. My tormentors emasculated me. They stripped me of my personhood. There I hung, naked for all to see.

Yes, I know what it's like to be exposed and humiliated.

## SELF-REFLECTION OR GROUP DISCUSSION

- The people involved in both Liz's and Jesus' exposure were insensitive to their suffering. Describe the insensitivity displayed by the people who abused you.

- Liz felt, to some degree, that she was responsible for what happened. How would you help Liz deal with her experiences? Describe any sense of blame you might feel for what happened to you. Why do you feel you're to blame?

- Fear of exposure is a big issue for many abuse survivors. Not just leftover fear from the fact that you were physically exposed and humiliated *at the time of the abuse*, but a terror that *who you really are* will also be exposed—that inner person you don't want anyone to see. When you think about exposure, what is it that terrifies you most?

- How can Christ's experiences of exposure help you find healing from your own experiences of exposure and humiliation?

# Surrounded by Cowards

## The Voice of Donna

What a fool I was! Expecting people to do the right thing, to protect me, to intervene! Not just one or two, but many, many people that I went to for help, to rescue me, to be my advocates. People I needed to stand by me, protect me, care enough about what happened to me—they were too spineless to risk standing up to the monster. My expectations were never met, and I hold every one of these cowards responsible for thirteen years of hell! To this day, I live with scars they—these impotent, disgusting, self-centered, passive abusers—helped create.

From ages five through eighteen, my stepfather sexually abused me. I told, and I told often, but nothing seemed to matter enough to end it. Those who could have stopped it or protected me from it thoroughly failed me.

When I was nine years old, charges were brought against my stepfather, and I was placed in a foster home. I had to do what no abuse victim wants to do, and certainly no child should have to do: I had to testify against him in court. I still have the court transcripts, but they are too painful for me to look at. The judge concluded that "white stuff" I talked about was not my stepfather's semen. I must have been mistaken or confused, he explained. The judge speculated that it was really calamine lotion, and he found my stepfather innocent! He then ordered me back home, sentenced to live with my mom and stepfather.

The judge could have stopped what was happening but chose not to.

By the time I was twelve, my mother regularly sent me in to pleasure my stepfather. My mother literally and actively sacrificed me to the evil dictator who was my stepfather. If I kept him happy, he was nice to my mom and she was nice to me. As if my own mother pimping me out wasn't enough, as if this reality weren't horrible enough, it created yet another dilemma. My mom used me to keep peace in the family, but she also viewed me, a twelve-year-old child, as "the other woman." Her competition!

My family was such a dysfunctional disaster that my siblings—even though they knew something very wrong was going on—actually thought I was the favored child! You see, one visit with him behind closed doors meant I got special favors, either for me or for someone else. My siblings often pressured me to ask my stepfather for privileges on their behalf. The cost? Sex with him. They despised me, yet they used me to get what they wanted from him. I felt as if they didn't love me, that they detested me and thought nothing of the price I paid for them.

When I was thirteen, I told the pastor of my church about the abuse. His only question to me was, "How do you know your stepfather is having sex with you?" I had to explain explicitly what was going on! This made me feel completely degraded and humiliated, even suspicious of him and why he needed to know those kinds of details. I left his office more confused than before I went in. I was desperately seeking someone to hear me, to do something, to make it stop. A few days later, the pastor requested I meet him in his office. Imagine my shock when I walked in to see my mother and stepfather already there, waiting for me! It was a complete setup. He gave my stepfather a good "talking to" and then explained that because he was having sex with me, he was suspended from being a Sunday school teacher. He said a prayer and sent me back to a few more years of hell on earth. My pastor did not use his moral obligations or his position of spiritual authority to protect me. In fact, the prayer he'd said became the religious sanction my stepfather needed to go unchecked as he systematically drained the life from me by his abuse.

My last attempt at finding someone with courage came when I was fifteen. My parents sent me to a private Christian school, and it was there that I told a teacher about the continuing abuse. His response? Well, it was obvious, according to him. I needed to pray more! So I prayed and I prayed and I prayed. While my friends were out enjoying free time, just being kids, this teacher had me in a small room praying. When no results occurred, when the abuse continued, he told me that I did not have enough faith. My teacher hid behind superficial religion and a shallow understanding of the depths of my pain. He would not get involved in any kind of meaningful way to help me escape the abuse. He refused to let the ugliness of my world invade his. He placed the consequences of false faith and false hope on my shoulders.

On *me* was placed the responsibility of my stepfather's actions. I carried my burden alone, surrounded by people who never exercised their power to protect me. No one did the right thing.

Jesus, do you know what it's like to be surrounded by cowards?

## The Voice of Jesus

Backroom deals and midnight trials were the only way these cowardly people could justify such a blatant misuse of power. Once the mob descended on me in the garden, it became a progressive parade of injustice. From dusk to dawn and into the next day, I was shuffled from one person to another: people with power, people who could orchestrate a cessation of the abusive whirlwind, people who did not do the right thing.

The Sanhedrin, Annas, and Caiaphas (the chief priest) were so nasty toward me it defied the imagination. Not only had they set a trap and used a trusted friend to do so, once they had me in their clutches, their hypocrisy and cruel contempt knew no bounds. Long before this moment, I had called them for what they were: whitewashed tombs with dead men's bones, vipers, a brood of snakes, hypocrites. But this was it, their moment to reveal themselves as malicious abusers of power who twisted the love of God until it mutated into an ugly, destructive force. These were my own people, not the Romans. My own people! They defiled their own faith traditions, broke their own laws, and hid behind a perversion of religion that could sacrifice innocent people in order to retain their places of power.

Not content with their own violence, I was hauled to the court of Governor Pontius Pilate. It was then that the elders and priests lost all restraint. These cowards, who were obviously very threatened by me and my message of love and peace, now aggressively challenged Pilate. They would not back down. They would not let go. It seemed they managed to find courage when their own agendas of power were at stake.

Pilate was not one of them. A Roman. A pagan. Not "one of us." He was annoyed and befuddled by this bizarre public display of religious bantering. Me—a poor man with no friends. Them—shouting and accusing me of such things as being God's child and a self-appointed king. Me—exhausted and broken. Them—smug, haughty, and arrogant. Me—aware of who and what I am. Pilate couldn't work through it, but he was certainly not going to rock the boat on my behalf.

A good beating should have appeased everyone, in his opinion. Well, I didn't deserve a beating, and he knew it. He just wanted the storm cloud of angry religious extremists to go away and thought my punishment would be received as a conciliatory act. His gesture had just the opposite effect. The mob became even more agitated. Things were getting out of control, and although he had the authority to put an end to this nonsense and rescue me, he didn't. In the grand picture, I didn't matter to him. I wasn't worth doing the right thing. He just wanted to get rid of everyone—to push "our" problem back into an invisible place he didn't have to see.

As the priests and elders chipped away at his apathetic treatment of me, it was disclosed that I was from Galilee. It was then that Pilate saw his exit strategy. This wasn't his problem. Galilee wasn't under his jurisdiction; it was under that of Herod Antipas, who happened to be in Jerusalem at the time, so off we went. The chief priests and elders risked losing control of this situation very quickly if Herod was not so quick to respond to their demands.

I was dehydrated, injured, and exhausted as the scorching desert sun baked my feeble skin. When our traveling show arrived before Herod, he became almost giddy. He knew of me. I was brought in to him for a private conversation. Seeker or merely in need of a little amusement I cannot say, but he had questions. I looked into the eyes of a man drunk with power and knew his fickle heart immediately. I was not going to waste my breath on this man. *Yes, I am who I say I am. No, I will not perform tricks for you.*

Those moments must have felt like an eternity for my waiting accusers. When we came out, he had me dressed in an elegant robe, his special way to belittle and humiliate me. The weight of it almost brought me to my knees, but at this point, I still had a bit of strength to stand. The best use he could find for all of his authority was to dress me like a show horse and back away from making a risky decision. Perhaps he was the most shallow and gutless of all. An odd sidebar to this was the impact of that robe on Pilate. He and Herod had been enemies, but when Herod returned me as a joke, they became good friends.

By this time, Pilate was wearing down. His wife had warned him not to condemn me. (At least one person in this chaotic scene attempted to use her power on my behalf.) In spite of her warnings, in spite of the false charges, in spite of the contradictory testimonies, in spite of the peculiar nature of the entire frenetic hysteria, he chose to be a coward.

By his own admission, he knew he was being manipulated. He knew I had done nothing wrong. He saw straight through them, saw this for what it was, yet he did not use the power he had to do the right thing. In the face of all the evidence, he symbolically washed his hands of the entire thing and quite literally signed my death sentence. I was returned to a mob that welcomed a murderer, Barabbas, and condemned me. I was innocent. They knew it. Herod knew it. Pilate knew it.

Every actor in this travesty had power. The Sanhedrin, Annas, Caiaphas, the elders and teachers, Pontius Pilate, Herod Antipas — they all had power. On me was placed the accusation of liars and the sentence of death. I carried my burden alone, overtaken by people who allowed it to happen. No one did the right thing.

Yes, I know what it's like to be surrounded by cowards.

## SELF-REFLECTION OR GROUP DISCUSSION

- Religious people who committed both Donna's and Jesus' abuse misused faith and their positions of spiritual authority. Civil authorities (teachers, officials, politicians, and the legal system) also misused their positions of power. Describe how those involved in your abuse misused faith or power, or both.

- Donna and Jesus were also failed by many people who had, perhaps, lesser degrees of power but still could influence the outcome. Describe the failures of those who could have used their influence to protect you.

- Injustice creates a very big injury for most abuse survivors. Christ experienced tremendous injustice throughout his life. What comfort or strength can you draw from that as you work on your abuse recovery?

# Godforsaken?

## *The Voice of Calvin*

The sermon was on God's love and power. Each word drove a wedge deeper and deeper between my faith and me. Is it love to be sexually abused? What good is God's power if a child cannot be protected? My abuser was more than happy to use her position in the church to manipulate and control me. I was just a boy, a little boy, when it began. This woman, Sister Lana we called her, taught our religious education classes. She took a great deal of interest in me, and my mother could not have been happier.

My mother was a devout Christian and my father was a devout drunk. My home was continually filled with tension and anger. Church was truly our sanctuary. At least it *had* been. I was quite young, perhaps six or seven, when her abuse began. I was the kid who came early and stayed late, anything to keep from going home. She picked up on this fact very quickly and showered affection and attention on my starving soul. I drank it in, and when I did, she had me right where she wanted me.

All the other children would quickly file out of the room after class, but I was usually asked to help Sister Lana with one thing or another. The church would empty and often there might be just the two of us in that big old building. That was how it began. She would escort me to the bathroom when I needed to go, and it was there that she exposed herself as I used the toilet. Her actions progressed with each bathroom trip until she finally molested me. She was my first sexual teacher, and what she taught opened up a world of perverted rage that took my adult life down a very dark path. I am still lost on that ugly path with no end in sight.

At first I was scared. I knew this was wrong, but she was so strong—physically and religiously—that I really had no option but to comply. Over the course of several months, the bathroom visits escalated, and the rituals she put me through both terrified and excited me. My little-boy body was doing just what God built it to do—feel arousal and pleasure—but the context of my pleasure was so twisted, so warped, that I could barely breathe. Just thinking about it right *now*, I can barely breathe. She threatened me with the fires of hell if anyone ever knew what I was doing "to" her, even though she was in her fifties and I was just a small child.

One day, the unthinkable happened. The janitor walked in on us, and Sister Lana screamed that I was trying to rape her. The janitor jerked me up off the bathroom floor by one arm and flung me up against the wall. Sister Lana was screaming at me and ran from the bathroom, securing her clothes and praying loudly, "O God! O God!" The next thing I knew, I was sitting on the back pew of the church with my hysterical mother and my drunken father, with Sister Lana putting on the performance of a lifetime in front of all of us and the pastor.

I was doomed, condemned, and punished in ways that still defy my imagination. My father, who had always been a brutal man, took it upon himself to become God's instrument of wrath, even though he had no use for God. From this point on, the beatings were so severe that I should have been hospitalized on many occasions if my dysfunctional family had not been so good at covering up the evidence. My mother, my hyperreligious mother, punished me by having me read chapter after chapter in the Bible every day and say my prayers for hours at a time.

Word quickly spread, and the other parents in our church

community shunned me. Sister Lana was still my religious education teacher, and she would publicly ridicule me in front of children and parents alike. The pastoral care I received involved long, loud ranting about the evils of sex and the evils of the body and that I was the Devil's child used to harm our dear Sister Lana. No one believed me. No one listened to me. No one understood all that had been taken from me.

I begged God to make it stop. It didn't. I begged God to kill my father. He didn't. I begged God to shut my mother up. He didn't. I begged God to bring me a friend. He didn't. I begged God to expose Sister Lana. He didn't. I begged God to kill me. He didn't, so I tried to do it for him.

My God, my God, why did you forsake me?

As a grown man, I am still alone. I am still condemned. I am a physical wreck, an emotionally stunted creature, a sexually twisted and addicted person. I feel as if God hates me. I thrash inside when I walk through the church doors. Yes, I still go to church. I try, I really do try, but I am so disconnected from God that I have no hope. I can't pray. I can't seek. I can't embrace faith. I am truly a man of despair, a man with no hope.

Jesus, do you know what it's like to feel godforsaken?

## The Voice of Jesus

I had done nothing wrong, yet here I was, my limbs stretched and nailed to beams of wood. I was naked, almost skinned alive, exhausted, dehydrated, and in shock. I was suspended between two thieves who were also being crucified. One lobbed as many slanders at me as my assassins had. The other man, broken beyond his body, gave me respect. The scenes of the preceding hours hit me with as much force as the nails that now held me in place. My mother, my friends, and my followers saw me in this condition and I worried for them; they would be traumatized by this horror. At the foot of my cross, gambling for my undergarments, soldiers took bets on when we'd all die.

The crowd still jeered, evidently not yet satisfied that my current condition was enough to fully degrade and emasculate me. Above my head, written in three languages, was a sign that identified my crime: "the king of the Jews." The shallow and ultimately cruel offering of sour wine could make no difference to me now. Every exquisite nerve I had fired rapid-sequence reminders to my brain that I was, indeed, human—that this pain was, indeed, experienced so fully as to become unbearable to me. It blinded me, deafened me.

From the depths of this agony, I howled so loudly I could almost hear my Father turn away. He did, in fact, do just that. I was alone with my accusers, surrounded by heinous lies, monstrous cruelty, and human failure. It was the first time in all of creation that I was no longer with my Father. I could not find him. I could not *feel* him. The terror and despair of *that* loomed so large that the horrific events of this wretched day diminished in contrast.

Even in the garden, I had asked my Father to let this ordeal bypass me, but that was not how it was to be. Now I was without Father God, plunged into darkness and left to face evil completely alone. That separation and darkness rippled across the ages until it caused the heavens to close in and the sky to turn black for hours. The air was stagnant and dead, the earth silent and shattered. Cut off from God, pain searing through every fiber of my being, I screamed with all of my might, "My God, my God, why have you forsaken me?"

I've felt the shock, the jarring awareness of being alone and unprotected. I've searched in frantic desperation for the parent of my soul and come up empty. I've clawed and fought and been overtaken by evil, reaching the end and finding there is still injustice, outrage, and pain waiting for me. Yes, I know what it's like to feel Godforsaken.

## SELF-REFLECTION OR GROUP DISCUSSION

- Both Calvin and Jesus felt as if they faced evil completely alone. Calvin's abuse brought a sense of deep spiritual injury to him. Describe how you felt, spiritually, when facing the evil of abuse.

- Jesus was there at the dawn of creation, and he will be there at the close. He knew the past, present, and future and yet desperately asked God where he was. What about that is surprising to you?

- Many abuse survivors feel condemned if they even entertain the thought that God abandoned them. Others feel great rage toward God or profound spiritual loss. Some have embraced faith as a great source of comfort, while others have turned away, or almost turned away, from God. Describe how your having been abused has impacted your spiritual journey.

- What do you think God the Father felt when Jesus cried out, "My God, my God, why have you forsaken me?"

# It Is Over

*The Voice of Mollie*

He had been the only one who'd ever said the words "I love you." He had been the only one who'd ever hugged me, ever knew I'd existed. He had been the one who'd taken me in. I was fed, clothed, and sheltered because of him. My parents were incapable of holding down jobs and could not take care of me, so I was shipped off to live with my grandparents. Here's the bitter truth: If it were not for my grandfather, I would have never been loved, never been provided for, never molested. He did all three.

His provisions came at a price—a price I had to pay or I'd be a homeless, abandoned child. He would molest me and then reward me. Molest. Reward. Molest. Reward. This toxic cycle continued until I was twelve years old.

My reward was always food—special treats of sugary desserts or fatty processed snacks. I learned at a very young age that food could bring me comfort. After each episode of his exploitation and violation, I sorely needed comfort. This meant I was fat. The brunt of cruel jokes at school. The scorn of the beautiful and svelte. Judged harshly by my peers and teachers as lazy and stupid. I was not. I just needed comfort. My weight packed insulation between my grandfather's abuse and my broken little-girl heart.

No one touched me but him. Everyone else was repulsed. I was the leper, and only he would take me as I was. Obese. Unwelcome. Unloved. Unwanted.

And then, just as I entered puberty, he died. The only person who ever told me "I love you" was gone. It would be another ten years before I heard those words again. The only person who cared for me was gone. The only person who exploited me was gone.

I stood over my grandfather's grave sobbing, uncontrollably sobbing. My family—my irresponsible parents, my submissive, silent grandmother, my brothers who taunted their fat sister for years—tried to console me, but I was not in need of comfort. My weeping was not that of a child grieving the loss of a beloved grandfather. It was not because I loved him that my tears fell. They fell out of relief, out of gratitude. You see, when he died, it was finally over.

Mine were the tears of liberation. Mine were tears of thanksgiving and the reckless worship of absolute certainty. The nightmare had an ending. My chubby face was red and swollen. My heavy body convulsed with joy, knowing that it would not be violated again by him. No one would ever love me like he did, and that reality sent me to my knees with praise.

Jesus, do you know what it's like to be relieved that it's finally over?

## The Voice of Jesus

The crowds had scattered. Unsettling things were taking place around the temple. Inside it, the heavy curtain that symbolized the separation between people and God would be torn in two as if it were a thin veil. Ground would shift beneath the feet of mortals. For now, my heart and body were broken beyond repair.

Horrid black skies hovered close. I was crowned with thorns, suspended on my throne of wood and nails. The darkness of inhumanity had run its course. Barbaric cruelty and unspeakable betrayal sat heavy like a stone rolled over my heart.

I had loved them. Loved them well. Walked their paths. Become a friend to them. Broke their bread and drank their wine. I'd opened their minds and enlightened their souls. But right now, at this moment, none of that mattered.

The tragic ending of my journey from Bethlehem to the Cross was now upon me. I would never be the same. Altered forever by this jarring experience of lack and loneliness and suffering. Too weak to breathe; each movement from my lungs expelled a bit more life from my body. A whiff. A wheeze.

I drew deeply from a well of wrenching sorrow—sorrow for all that was, all that had been. With one last breath, I said, "It is finished." And then there was peace. Yes, I was filled with relief that it was finally over.

## SELF-REFLECTION OR GROUP DISCUSSION

- Abuse may end with childhood, but the complications or damage rarely end. It is important to separate those two things: the actual abuse and the residual damage. What about your abuse has ended? What continues?

- Sometimes the grief survivors feel is not only about the actual abuse or even the abuser but also over what they never had, the person that their abuser never was, the childhood that they never had, the innocence that left too soon. What is over that you grieve for now? What is over that you rejoice because of?

- Mollie felt relief at her grandfather's funeral. Jesus' statement "It is finished" came at the end of a very long ordeal. It wasn't neat and tidy. It was a roller coaster of emotion, pain, joy, and sorrow. Describe what your recovery journey looks like as well as what it needs to look like in order for you to say those same words, "It is finished."

# Rediscovering Life

## The Voice of Ethan

Fifteen years had passed since my uncle had abused me. Now, at the age of twenty-six, I sat in his living room with the rest of our family waiting to leave for his funeral. He died of the same disease I now have, the one he gave me: HIV/AIDS.

I heard the funeral service from the bottom of a deep, black hole in my mind. Everything felt pushed away and filtered through my distant places of time and pain. Words and phrases drifted through this hollow cavern until the sounds of weeping people settled down there with me. They spoke of a man I did not recognize—a man I never knew. The man I knew was different from the one for whom they grieved. The man I knew violated my trust, my body, and my future.

This dark enclave was a familiar place in which I often dwelled. Long seasons of depression. Extended periods of isolation. Torturous rage. A life-shattering disease. These were what remained of his cold, empty legacy. This was his memorial within me.

The casket was opened. We filed by, looking at a facade. Even in death, I was sure his eyes would pop open as I stared down and that haunting voice of his would plead with me once more, "Don't tell, please don't tell." And you know, I never did. On to the cemetery our little group of mourners snaked. There, one by one, we tossed a handful of dirt into the hole where his body now rested in peace. I envied that thought—to rest in peace. I lived on, in torment.

Family and friends hugged each other, comforted each other, left the fresh grave piled high with dirt and flowers. Everyone moved on. Life, it seems, does go on under some circumstances, but not for me. I couldn't move past the abuse. I couldn't be normal because of my disease. I couldn't be free because of the murky secrets and my deep depression.

A few months passed and I decided to return to my uncle's grave. His gravestone was now in place, and a bench was set close by. I was drawn to it and sat. The epitaph for this man, the one who put me into a place of such bleak despair, read,

Here Lies Our Son, Brother, Uncle, and Friend
Light of Our Lives, Joy of Our Hearts

My body convulsed in pain. My soul agonized in silence. I glared at that grave, believing that somehow this monument to my uncle would bring closure for me. A soft breeze caressed my face, accompanied by the sweet smell of nearby honeysuckle. I waited. Waited for finality. Waited for hope. Waited to *be*.

As I waited, a bright red cardinal landed on the gravestone and chirped another distant bird's song to life. The air filled with their duet and he flew toward that song. My eyes followed his flight away from that grave. My uncle was gone. I could sit in that cemetery until I joined him in the ground, but it occurred to me that this was not the place where I would ever find answers or closure.

With my eyes, I followed that cardinal beyond the cemetery. With my soul, I heard his song, which beckoned me to stop looking for life in places of death.

Jesus, is it possible to rediscover life?

## The Voice of Jesus

I emerged with no pain. The sensation of calm and wholeness vividly contrasted what I had last known in this body just three days earlier. I still had scars, still had memories, but the horror of those moments was now part of my history—now part of the history of the world. I was escorted back by several celestial friends as the dawn awaited my return. This was to be a very full day—a day of surprises and reunions, a day of restoration and proof, a day of enlightenment and revelation, a day when the familiar would finally make sense.

Throughout this day, I would walk with my followers and yet they wouldn't recognize me. I would have to retell my stories in the context of my death and resurrection and then wait for them to see me again for the first time. I would have to break bread and pour wine, then watch the familiarity of my actions slowly reveal who I am, right before their eyes. I would have to move into their locked-up rooms of fear and self-preservation, then steady their nerves while they adjusted to a new reality. I would have to require the doubters to touch me and convince the hungry that I, too, was hungry.

I would speak their names, breathe my life into their spirits, comfort their traumatized minds. I would point them in a new direction and remind them of what they already knew: that I am the Christ.

All of this lay ahead of me on this new day. A strong earthquake shook the large tombstone loose and I walked out, back into the sunlight—back into the lives of my disciples.

"Wait for them," I instructed the angels, knowing that some of my frightened followers would be here soon.

They had been traumatized, terrorized, and abandoned. More questions than answers pressed hard against their shattered hearts. This was the condition in which several of them arrived at my empty tomb. They became hysterical. They tore through the tomb's opening, groping in the dark for my body, only to find empty grave clothes but not me. Two angelic beings illuminated the tomb's interior, which terrified my friends even more. With strength and comfort, the angels revealed the truth to these precious ones of what lies beyond the tragedies of human cruelty. Then they asked a pointed question, one I'd instructed them to ask: "Why do you look for the living among the dead?"

Life returned to my dead body. Soon it would return to my dear ones who thought that all was lost. You see, dear one, life can be rediscovered, but not in the dead places. Beyond them.

## SELF-REFLECTION OR GROUP DISCUSSION

- Both Ethan and Jesus emerged from the terrible legacy of abuse with life and vitality. Describe what you think will be involved in order for you to do the same.

- Most abuse survivors try many avenues and experiences in their quest to find answers or closure. Sometimes those avenues have been in dead things, such as self-destructive behavior or actions harmful to others. Sometimes the recovery process can bring about life, such as a great spiritual awakening or a new way of viewing yourself. Identify those times in your pursuit of healing when you sought life in dead things. What were the consequences (for you or others) from your doing so?

- Jesus was very concerned that his followers would stop their journey at his empty tomb. He knew that in that place they would only stagnate. It is easy to get stuck in abuse recovery, but if you don't continue the journey beyond dead things, you will stagnate. What do you see as a danger to your continued journey, and what steps do you need to take in order to move forward and follow life?

# Clothed with Power

*The Voice of Eric*

I sat with dignity, strength, and courage. I spoke with respect, experience, and compassion. I was clothed and clean and strong. I was no longer my abuser's victim. I was a survivor—one who overcame.

Before me was a group who had gathered to find their own healing. To these precious people, I bore testimony to what was done. I did not falter. I did not wince. The lies were silenced and the truth was revealed. "These are the things I endured," I said. "These are the lies I believed. This is the damage that was done."

Years before this, I was where this group now sat: at a retreat for abuse survivors. I was traumatized, ashamed, enraged, and addicted. I cowered and thrashed and resisted the truth. In a setting just like this one, I stormed out of the group session and found a tree upon which I pounded my fist again and again and again, screaming at God and my memories and the tree. My hand didn't shatter that day, but the hard outer layers of my abuse cracked open just a bit—just enough for a tiny sliver of life to filter through to my dark pain and give me my first taste of freedom.

I spent most of my twenties recovering from my horrific childhood. I had been raped, beaten, and degraded, but here I was, sharing hope with fellow abuse survivors. The student had become the teacher. The hard labor had brought life from death. Mine had been a relentless pursuit of truth and clarity. The disciplined practices of using my voice, honoring myself, and establishing boundaries had come to fruition.

I have come this far because I refused to believe that my entire life must be defined by what my abusers did to me. I have come this far because I wouldn't let them win; I wouldn't let them have any more of me than what they had already taken. I have come this far because I discovered commonality with a suffering Christ. A God who put on an earth-suit just like mine and was perfected through the experience of suffering. I have come this far because I have One who has gone before me, endured things so similar to my own abuse, yet he never became like those who committed the horrible acts against him. I won't either.

I have come this far because I chose peace over rage, love over hate, compassion over cruelty, and dignity over degradation. I have followed Christ beyond what was done to me, and through that process, I have discovered who we both are: clean and covered.

I am who I am today because I am no longer that naked, shivering little boy. I am who I am because I am clothed with power — the power of love, joy, and peace. I am the righteousness of Christ.

## The Voice of Jesus

I gathered them one last time. One last meal. One last embrace. One last conversation. I was strong, having recovered from my mortal wounds. And, yes, I was also scarred. That's what time on this planet does to you — it scars you. Some scars are deeper than others, and mine were very, very deep.

All the risks I had taken to open my heart, to become weak and vulnerable, to suffer from physical harm and relational failure, had been worth the sacrifice. I had walked through the human experience. I had not skipped a step nor placed myself above suffering. I had known pain as only a human being can know it and it did not conquer me; it emboldened me to keep the way of escape open for them.

I had been where they were now. Standing on the precipice of the unknown, I looked into the face of barbaric cruelty and uncertainty, not sure of what my experiences would feel like. I had not taken the easy way out and I did not shrink from any part of the human experience. Had I done so, the path I forged for them would not be complete — not be authentic.

They were special, these friends of mine. They now hung on my every word, recognizing that what I knew, they would know. Where I had been, they were right now. Where I was going, they would be able to follow.

It was a strange good-bye. It wasn't filled with the heart-wrenching sorrow of our last meal together more than forty days ago. I had pushed the boundaries of tragedy and pushed through to the open sky of new life. They could do the same.

Only a few years ago, I had invited them to follow me. They had. Because I broke through the walls of anger, hatred, exploitation, and abuse, they, too, could continue following me to a life beyond those things.

It was imperative that they not follow me alone. Others, both now and throughout the centuries to come, would find themselves trapped with no means of escape. The good news of this hidden passage to freedom now rested on my followers. They knew the way because I knew the way.

There is life beyond suffering. There is something beyond being exposed, degraded, exploited, and harmed. One last time, I looked into each one's eyes.

"I'm leaving you now, but not leaving you as I found you. I'm taking up residence in a place of permanence; I'm moving into your heart. This means you will never be without me. You will never walk alone. You will do exactly as I have done: you will overcome. Things are hard, of that we are all certain, but I am now entrusting you with the good news that there's more than this.

"My precious friends, you are no longer exposed. You are clothed with power from on high. This is my parting gift to you until we meet again."

And with that, clothed with power that was always mine to use, I pushed the gate fully open and invited them to follow me.

## Self-Reflection or Group Discussion

- Eric saw himself differently than he had at the beginning of his recovery journey. What changes have you noticed in yourself as you have examined Christ's experiences with abuse?

- Christ did not "skip a step" in his journey through suffering and abuse. How can this understanding help your faith as you move through the issues of your own abuse?

- Christ took his experiences one step further after his ordeal. He created a new path beyond suffering and injustice, which abuse survivors can follow too. Rather than hate, he showed love. Rather than abusing his own power, he used it to comfort and guide. Rather than rage, he demonstrated peace. In following Christ beyond your own abuse, what can you find in his example that will help you counter and conquer the suffering and injustice you have experienced?

# What This Means

Have you felt completely alone as you struggle with all the damage that remains from abuse? The shock of being set up and betrayed. The terrifying sense of abandonment, exposure, and humiliation. The dread that still lurks near every dark shadow and unknown path. The gut-wrenching realization that cowards wouldn't protect you. The aching sense that God, too, has forsaken you. This isolation may keep you sifting through the debris as you frantically search for life in dead places. If that's where you had to remain, the possibility of complete despair might keep that stone firmly in place over your broken dreams. But it's not.

You're not alone. That's the point of this book—to give you a glimpse into the life of Christ in a way that empowers you on your spiritual journey away from abuse. I hope doing so helps you embrace your commonality, or shared experiences, of suffering and abuse with Christ. Christ, as our "Wonderful Counselor" (Isaiah 9:6), becomes one who skillfully listens to your stories with understanding and acceptance.

Commonality has the potential to completely change the connection dynamics you have with God. It moves communication to an entirely different plateau since it is unnecessary to explain terms, describe sensations, or defend your responses. Christ, who has experienced suffering, can truly empathize with what you've been through. This commonality is where we begin to piece the puzzle together so that Christ's life on earth can change *your* life on earth!

I hope you're beginning to hear the voice of God (see Hebrews

1:2) that speaks deeply to your own story of suffering. Of course, suffering was not a surprise to God. Just by sheer observation, God was acutely aware that his perfect world had become a wretched place. But do you realize that for God, something was missing? Something was lacking—the actual experience of suffering. It was the lack of experience that motivated God to put on an earth-suit and become one of us.

Because Christ stepped into human history as he did, his understanding of suffering became complete. Hebrews 2:10 says, "It was fitting that God, for whom and through whom everything exists, should make the author of their salvation perfect through suffering." In other words, it was the experience of suffering that perfected Christ.

This effort by Christ was not easy. It was difficult and painful, just as yours was. Hebrews 2:18 explains that "because he himself suffered when he was tempted, he is able to help those who are being tempted." Every cell and emotion of what it means to be part of the human family was experienced by Christ. No special favors. No magic pain relievers. He experienced raw, fire-breathing life in all its glory and heartache.

If you grew up attending church, you learned from childhood that Jesus came to die for the sins of the world. While that is a true statement, it is not a complete statement. It misses one of the major reasons for his mission: to have the human experience.

Think about it. If the only reason for Christ's appearing was atonement (paying for the sins of the world), then Jesus could have been slaughtered with all of the baby boys in Bethlehem (see Matthew 2:13-18) and his mission would have been accomplished. At that moment, atonement would have been complete. This fact tells us that there was more to Christ's mission than to offer atonement for sin.

Between our songs that celebrate Christmas and those that solemnly remember Good Friday, there is a profound message from God to humanity. It is a message that often eludes us because it is so obvious. Confined to a womb, experiencing the birth process, through infancy, childhood, adolescence, and adulthood, Jesus was human. He died in a brutal way that involved intimate relationships, genital exposure, and prolonged pain inflicted by cruel people. These experiences place Christ in the role of mediator between spirit and flesh.

A mediator is a go-between — someone who helps bring two parties together to find common ground, create understanding, and restore or ensure peace. This certainly describes the role Christ now fills between God and people. He comes from both worlds and offers the opportunity to find common ground, understanding, and peace. Because of this, you are encouraged to pursue this cosmic dynamic with aggressive boldness, assured that you will be accepted, understood, and accurately represented. The author of Hebrews 4:14-16 affirms this by concluding,

> Therefore, since we have a great high priest who has gone through the heavens, Jesus the Son of God, let us hold firmly to the faith we profess. For we do not have a high priest who is unable to sympathize with our weaknesses, but we have one who has been tempted in every way, just as we are — yet was without sin. Let us then approach the throne of grace with confidence, so that we may receive mercy and find grace to help us in our time of need.

In other words, Christ empathizes and identifies with your weaknesses because he experienced many of the same struggles you've experienced. Jesus suffered when he struggled, yet he was strong enough to overcome those struggles and, by doing so, left you an example to follow. Because Jesus actually experienced pain and abuse, something powerful happens when you pray.

Visualize this picture when you think about prayer: Jesus takes your hand, the hand of flesh, and takes the hand of God, the hand of Spirit, and begins to translate your experiences through his own. He tells his Father what it felt like to be abandoned, exposed, shamed, humiliated, afraid, and hurt. Jesus translates the human experience into divine terms and then joins these two worlds (human and divine) together to bring about peace and restoration. Jesus literally joins flesh with spirit to make spiritual healing possible. You are connected to God at the place of your deepest pain, fear, humiliation, and shame. This is our sacred commonality.

As you consider the suffering of Christ, there is one point that must be carefully understood. Some people look at what happened to Jesus and think that God victimized his own son. This is a false idea that could not be further from the truth. The words of Christ, as recorded in John 10:17-18, are unambiguous: "The reason my Father loves me is that I lay down my life—only to take it up again. No one takes it from me, but I lay it down of my own accord. I have authority to lay it down and authority to take it up again." Jesus made it very clear that he was not a victim. Jesus was a volunteer who chose to experience the human condition in order to be a credible mediator.

The role of Christ as mediator—fellow abuse survivor, both mortal and divine—creates the opportunity for you to move from a place of isolation to a place of inclusion and truth. Christ's own rite of passage was difficult and treacherous. As a result, he cleared the debris from your path and opened up your personal rite of passage. He empowers you to find your way to a place of healing and dignity.

## Self-Reflection or Group Discussion

- Describe how your commonality with Christ can change how you communicate with God.
- What is your reaction to the statement that "lack of experience that motivated God to put on an earth-suit and become one of us"?
- What would we have missed if Christ had been slaughtered as a baby in Bethlehem?
- Christ was not a victim of a God-conspiracy; he made the choice to have the human experience. In doing so, he became a credible mediator. Think about the role Christ plays as mediator between flesh and spirit. What do you think you would hear him say on your behalf as you pray about your abuse and recovery?

# What to Do

## *The Voice of the Author*

I clearly remember the moment I became a follower of Christ. I had taken ownership for my mistakes, made some tough choices to change how I lived, and asked God to forgive my sins. As I think back, one of the things that stands out to me was the tremendous sense of relief from guilt that I felt. I felt as light as a helium-filled balloon, like an eagle released back into the wild, or, like Atlas from Greek mythology, finally relieved of carrying the world on his shoulders. I felt clean and pure. In Christian terms, I was "born again," given another chance, a place to start over, a new place to begin.

When I began my spiritual journey through abuse recovery, I found myself hitting a wall that I couldn't seem to break through. It was the wall of false guilt and false shame, placed there by my abuser. I was able to sift through the facts and knew I wasn't responsible for what had happened, but that shame — that awful shame — was still there. Spiritually, I didn't know what to do with it. I couldn't repent because the sin wasn't mine to repent of, yet the shame from my abuser's sin left me feeling defiled and filthy. It left me searching to discover how God fit into this very real dilemma. In my search, I discovered a mechanism, a principle, in Scripture that changed my life. I call it "spiritual hygiene." Before we look at spiritual hygiene, let me frame some ideas that will help you understand it.

## Looking at the Past

The lies from the past can tell you that you are still filthy, even if you are working to become a spiritually healthy person. You may find yourself convinced that you are not worthy of being loved. You may believe that your ugly, twisted scars are the only things people see when they look at you. The fact is that God sees you in a completely different way. God sees you with absolute truth and totally pure love. Consider these statements:

- God knows that you were a victim of abuse and that it was not your fault. Even if there was pleasure experienced or compensation given, God is well aware of who is responsible for the abuse: your abuser.

- God knows what you see in your mind and remember. Whether you acknowledge this or not, God is well aware of what lives in your mind's eye. The flashbacks, the twisted thoughts, the chaos and rage are not surprising to God. God is right there with you, seeing your memories and knowing your thoughts. In light of this, God has the power to clean your mind, body, and spirit. None of this is beyond God's ability.

- God knows that you have been left feeling filthy, defiled, damaged, and tainted. The emotional responses to abuse are understood by him. He recognizes the debris of false guilt and false shame for what they are. God also understands that this damage extends to your relationships with him and with other people.

- God loves you in spite of all you have seen and done. No depth of depravity, no experience or sensation, no gain or loss can stop God from loving you. It is simply impossible for God not to love those he created (see Romans 8:35-39).

- What happened in the past cannot be changed. You have

memories and pain that are part of your life. No amount of compensation or denial will change that reality. While your personal history cannot be erased, that does not imply that you must remain enslaved by it. The journey of abuse recovery with Christ doesn't cause you to be emotionally neutered; however, the possibility of becoming emotionally clear and purified is very real.

## Spiritual Hygiene

God is profoundly aware of your need to be liberated from false shame. He has provided a practical mechanism for your spiritual emancipation, which can enable you to be released from the damage you carry. This mechanism can be found in 1 John 1:5-9. It is written this way:

> *This is the message we have heard from him and declare to you: God is light; in him there is no darkness at all. If we claim to have fellowship with him yet walk in the darkness, we lie and do not live by the truth. But if we walk in the light, as he is in the light, we have fellowship with one another, and the blood of Jesus, his Son, purifies us from* all *sin.*
>
> *If we claim to be without sin, we deceive ourselves and the truth is not in us. If we confess our sins, he is faithful and just and will forgive us our sins and purify us from* all *unrighteousness.* (emphasis added)

Abuse is sin and it causes damage to its victim. You, as an abuse survivor, live with the damage caused by someone else's sin. First John 1:5-9 explains what to do with sin, both yours and your abuser's. I want to make it very clear that our focus right now is on your need to find spiritual cleansing from the false shame and guilt imposed upon you by your abuser. This passage of Scripture indicates that Jesus can cleanse and purify you from *all* sin and *all* unrighteousness. Not just your sin but *all* sin is included in Christ's power to bring relief and release.

Confession is simply the act of telling the truth. Repentance and confession are not necessarily the same things. Repentance means that you accept responsibility for what is contained in the truth you are confessing. In this context, I am not referring to repentance. It is important to note that when you are telling the truth about what was done to you during the abuse, God does not in any way hold you responsible for those experiences. With this clearly understood, knowing that God will never hold you responsible for sins committed against you, it is equally certain that God can cleanse you from the false shame caused by others' sins.

As you follow the instructions of 1 John 1:5-9, you speak the truth to God (tell God what happened to you), acknowledge the damage that has resulted from that truth, and ask for decontamination of false shame and guilt.

It is important to recognize why abuse holds so much power over you. Abuse is not just a one-dimensional series of events on a timeline; it is an experience that includes sights, sounds, smells, textures, temperatures, relationships, fear, pleasure, pain, power, and many other sensations. All of these create false shame. This causes abuse to have a multidimensional impact on you. It delivers a one-two punch that causes extensive harm.

The energy that gives abuse so much power is not simply your timeline story, with the facts laid out in a linear fashion; it is this multidimensional factor, charged with shame and secrecy, from which you must find release. Frequently, those sensations and experiences are what you are most terrified of sharing with other people. It's one thing to tell someone you were abused; it's quite another to add that your first experience with sexual pleasure happened then too. In truth, the problem is not with sexual pleasure; the problem is the context in which that pleasure occurred. But it is that kind of admission that keeps us isolated in false guilt.

In the reality of your private shame, you will discover that the truth of 1 John 1:5-9 can become an important step in finding spiritual healing and emotional cleansing. This is how spiritual hygiene works, as laid out in that passage:

- One memory at a time—be it the actual events or the sensations, consequences, and responses associated with them—tell God every detail you can remember. This is "confessing," or telling the truth to God. Tell God the truth about your abuser's sins.
- You do not need to ask God to forgive you of your abuser's sins, as you cannot repent of someone else's sins. That is not your responsibility, so don't take ownership of someone else's guilt.
- Ask God to cleanse and purify you from this damage (false shame) because of your abuser's sins.
- Do this whenever these memories attack you, and do it as often as you need to.

By practicing spiritual hygiene, you will become skilled at embracing truth and shedding shame. As with any other practice in life, the more you do something, the better you become at it. The better you become at something, the more results you see. By allowing God to release you from *all* unrighteousness, you take a big step away from the darkness and power of your abuse. You take your life away from your abusers and return it to yourself and God. You move from darkness to light. Because God is light, you take up residence with light too.

One dilemma you may face is your frequent struggle with the same memories over and over. This is when you must be especially determined to practice spiritual hygiene. Perhaps well-meaning people have told you not to take the same issues to God more than once. They imply that if you do so, you do not have faith. This is simply not true. The truth is that God has a deep desire for you to come to him with anything that bothers you. This is true for flashbacks as well as distorted emotions. When these resurface, take them to God once more and ask him to help you find peace.

No matter how many times you have spoken the truth to God about a memory or an issue, God wants you to come to him. The invitation extended by Christ in Matthew 11:28 is not a onetime invitation. Christ said, "Come to me, all you who are weary and burdened, and I will give you rest." This is ongoing and open-ended.

God urges you to openly and honestly come to him with your truth and your thoughts. Christians sometimes play the mental game of "I shouldn't be feeling this way" or "I shouldn't be thinking this." The fact is, regardless of whether you should or shouldn't—if you do, you do! You will either go to God with it or you will not. God urges you to come to him as many times as you need to with any issue that concerns you.

This concept of repetition can be thought of in the same way as washing your hands. You wash them when they get dirty. The next time they are dirty, you will wash them again. No one thinks less of you for it. God invites you to repeat the process of spiritual hygiene as often as you need to. There is nothing wrong with taking your memories and thoughts to God until you feel a release from the false shame and guilt. This is how you practice spiritual hygiene.

By honestly bringing God into your memories, thoughts, responses, and pain, you can effectively redirect your mind and spirit to dwell on personal freedom and healthy ideas. You enlist his help to expose the lies, and, by doing so, you will gradually find release from the power that these thoughts and flashbacks have over you.

Spiritual hygiene takes time. It is a practice that requires discipline, repetition, and a realignment of your pain with Christ. Facilitated through meditation and prayer, you will gradually exchange the lies of abuse for the truth of Christ's love and freedom.

# Self-Reflection or Group Discussion

- First John 1:5-9 indicates that Christ has the power to purify us from *all* sin and *all* unrighteousness. This includes the false shame and guilt that most abuse survivors struggle with. Spiritual hygiene involves using the concepts found in 1 John 1:5-9, which involve speaking the truth and asking God to cleanse and purify you of that truth's consequences. How do you think this can set you free from false guilt and false shame?

- Most abuse survivors repeatedly struggle with the same issues and memories. The good news is that God will never grow weary of your coming to him with these again and again. What you think and feel is not to be ignored. What do you see as being the biggest obstacle in taking your thoughts, feelings, impulses, and memories to God?

- How do you think the practice of spiritual hygiene can facilitate your journey beyond abuse?

# An Audience of One

The essence of counseling is that you bear witness to your experiences, and a listener (the counselor) receives that testimony. You speak it, and the counselor hears it. You share it with another. The listener must be skilled to assist you as you strategically maneuver through your past and the damage that resulted from it. In other words, you invest your time, money, and energy to have an audience of one.

I am a strong proponent of counseling. The issues that remain after childhood abuse can roll around in your head for years and get so tangled and confused that you do not have the clarity or perspective to untie the knots by yourself. The audience of one is a powerful solution to that dilemma, and I encourage you to find a good counselor who can help you. There is a reference at the end of this book to help you search for a counselor who is right for you. The bottom line is you need to use your voice in such a way that it is heard by another. Who that "another" is may be a licensed counselor, a clergyperson, a good friend, your partner, or a member of your family.

That being said, I want to give you something else to consider as you ponder this important step. In the early days of my initial counseling, I would sit for that precious one hour with my therapist and find I could not talk. I would get so frustrated with myself. At best, I would get out only a few sentences when I got deeper into my pain and experiences. I watched the clock tick and my silence pour through that time like sand in an hourglass. It was common for me to fight my way through the shame and fear to find the courage to speak just as our time was up. I had to leave because another shattered soul was in the waiting room, hoping to find his words that needed to be spoken and heard. I felt as if I were burning money. Of course, if you've gone through counseling, you know this is normal, but all I could hear was the cash register ringing as each quiet minute ticked by. It was often on my drive home that the words finally came—the ones I needed to share, the ones that seemed too difficult to utter at the time.

There were periods of time when I needed an audience of one in the middle of the night to listen and help—moments during church or grocery shopping or showering or sex when important words from the past needed to be spoken and heard but were not. You see, the reality is that even if you find the greatest therapist on the planet, he or she cannot always be there to receive your words and guide you through what they might mean. A therapist isn't always available to help you solve an issue or determine an appropriate course of action.

The luxury of having a therapist on call twenty-four/seven is simply not possible. Even if you are institutionalized, you will not have instant access to your therapist. He is, after all, human. He eats, sleeps, gets sick, takes vacations, and has a life outside of his practice. If he doesn't, you need to find someone new, and he needs to find his own professional help! But what do you do with those off-hour epiphanies? What do you do when you need to tell another piece of the story, when a bit more light has pushed through the dark pit of despair, when you wake with your heart in your throat because the monster has snagged you one more time? Where is your skilled audience of one then?

People of faith are empowered to do something with this dilemma. One of the glaring truths many abuse survivors miss is the ever-present presence of God's Spirit. No matter where you are, what time it is, or what you need, God is there. To get a better sense of this, consider the following: If I am alone in a room and my husband, Tim, comes in, I can do one of two things. I can turn, smile, and say hi, or I can ignore him. If I ignore him, is he any less in the room than if I acknowledge his presence? Of course not! He is there, regardless of how I respond.

The same is true of God. He is with you. Whether you speak or are silent, the room is occupied by One more than you.

The application of this idea with your need to be heard can have a profound impact on your personal journey beyond abuse. Write your memories, insights, and issues to God. Speak your story to God. Scream your anger to God. Paint your sorrow to God. Dance your pain to God. Sing your heart to God. The point is that you do all of these things *to* a hearer, to a listener, to God. You acknowledge that he is in the room, and you rely on his listening. You use your voice, in whatever form you choose, and entrust your words, emotions, and issues to an audience of One. Twenty-four/seven. Reasonable fees. Instant access. No appointment necessary.

Talk it out. Talk it through. Talk it over and over and over. Your audience of One is in the room, ready, willing, and able to listen. Your audience of One has the wisdom, skills, insights, and strategies to help you make progress on your journey. After all, Jesus said in John 16:13-15,

> When he, the Spirit of truth, comes, he will guide you into all truth. He will not speak on his own; he will speak only what he hears, and he will tell you what is yet to come. He will bring glory to me by taking from what is mine and making it known to you. All that belongs to the Father is mine. That is why I said the Spirit will take from what is mine and make it known to you.

This truth reaches beyond tools for evangelism or charismatic gifts. This truth empowers you to know that your counselor is skilled. The Spirit of truth is ready for you, willing to listen to you, and able to guide you to a healthier place.

The beautiful thing about God, your audience of One, is that his hearing is perfect and his wisdom is far-reaching. What you hear from God will complement the hearing you receive from your mortal audience of one—your counselor, pastor, or friend. In fact, your human counselor has worked hard to acquire the appropriate skills and knowledge to help you. That wisdom is also from God. Truth is truth. Do not be hesitant to use whatever avenue you need in order to find that truth. During normal office hours, perhaps your audience of one will be your therapist, supervised by the Spirit of truth. In the middle of the night, your audience of One sits in the chair, providing comfort, a listening ear, and vision far beyond the night's darkness. Either way, your audience of One is still there.

## SELF-REFLECTION OR GROUP DISCUSSION

- When you use your voice to tell your stories, you are using it to connect with others. The reality is that it is impossible for someone to always be there when you need a person to talk to. Can you think of a time when you really needed someone to talk to but there was no one there for you? What did that need feel like? What did you do to meet that need?

- God's Spirit is ever-present with you, always ready to hear you, to compassionately and experientially listen to your stories, to be your audience of One, even in the middle of the night or during the middle of church. How can you take advantage of God's ever-present Spirit in your abuse recovery?

- Truth is truth. What are your thoughts about this statement, and how can it help you when you consider following the guidance of human counselors?

- In counseling, your testimony is received by another who has the skills to help you navigate through confused thinking and behavior. In those times when you do not have access to a human audience, you still have access to truth. Consider the teachings of John 16:13-15. What assurances do you have regarding your need for clarification and guidance?

# To Follow Christ

The issues of injustice are paramount to any abuse survivor: the taking of innocence, the ruining of a childhood and oftentimes an entire lifetime, the awareness that most perpetrators go without being exposed or punished, the conflict of emotions toward the people involved in the abuse. The harsh realization is that the one who is left with the damage, the one who must fight unfair battles, the one who must spend more energy, more time, and more money to recover is you—these are the outrageous injustices for most abuse survivors. Even if your abuser is incarcerated, exposed, and publicly chastised for his or her actions, the injustices you must deal with are very real and very powerful. No matter how high a price your offender pays, you pay the higher price. Take a deep breath; that's reality.

It is not the scope of this book to tackle the issue of forgiveness, and there are many wonderful teachers and books that can articulate this important area better than I can, but there are some thoughts about it that I want to share. One thing I teach regarding forgiveness is that it is an act of decision making. The forgiveness decision each of us must reach is that of releasing. You release yourself from the penalty that someone else's actions have imposed upon you. People of faith take this act of releasing a step further by releasing these experiences of injustice to God. It is on God's shoulders that people who forgive squarely place the responsibilities of justice. If you don't trust God or don't believe in God, you can still make a decision to release yourself, but people of faith not only release themselves but also release the issues of justice *to* someone: God.

During a Committed to Freedom retreat several years ago, I was teaching a session on forgiveness. We were looking at various ideas about forgiveness, including the idea that no matter how bitter we are, we cannot change the historical events in our lives. So many of us spend enormous amounts of energy fighting the past but never resolve that it is a historical fact, a part of your timeline, a tragic episode in your past. One retreat participant gasped and said, "So you're telling me that I am still fighting a war that is over—and I lost." I'd never put it that way before, but that was fairly accurate. In fact, it is basically the productive beginning of abuse recovery: acceptance.

Not approval. Acceptance. Not condoning. Acceptance. Not confrontation, compensation, or forgetting. Acceptance. Once you acknowledge what happened to you in the deep interiors of your soul, you'll be working with reality. Then you can use all of your precious energy to move beyond abuse rather than continue fighting a war that is over. You may have lost that round of battle, but you do not have to lose any more ground. It is in this truth that you begin.

As you read this book and recognize how your voice is connected with Christ's, I want to wrap these ideas together into a package you can carry: how to follow Christ through your recovery. As we look to the life of Christ on this planet, in his earth-suit, there is a progression I hope you can see. It will help you recognize that the trail has already been broken. The way is cleared for you because of Christ's transparent journey. If you look for it, you will begin to see it for yourself and know what to do with all of the injustices you've suffered.

When I speak of following Christ, I am not speaking evangelistically. That, too, is reserved for another book or sermon or spiritual epiphany. I mean you literally *follow* the path of Christ in your recovery journey. You follow his suffering, his realities, his isolation and misuse, and the past that he conquered, which moved him from death back to life.

Christ suffered. No free passes or magic tricks. He suffered. He was violated with a kiss, betrayed by those he loved, and abandoned by those he trusted. He was stripped naked, degraded, and brutally attacked by those who had power. He was the object of bigoted hatred, rage, and evil. He was failed by his faith community. His civil rights and due process were completely thrown out the window and disregarded. He was humiliated and mocked. He was tortured and ignored. He was discarded without mercy. As you walk through your own suffering, look up and follow Christ through his. You follow a fellow abuse survivor who suffered as you have suffered. In doing so, you begin to know that you are understood by One with common experiences, One whose feet are planted in both the physical and the spiritual realms, One who understands with an empathy that includes scars very much like yours. Christ suffered. You suffered. You both understand what that means.

Christ faced harsh realities. Once the events that led up to his crucifixion were over, he was left alone, suspended in his suffering, waiting to die. His body was exhausted, exploited, and broken. His heart was more shattered than his flesh. He languished in pain and no one showed him mercy. Even as he suffered from the wounds that had been inflicted, his tormentors continued to degrade him. They gambled for his clothes right before his eyes, right before his traumatized body. It was yet another insult to the injuries they'd caused. No respect, no regard, no compassion.

The impact of these experiences was so profound that Christ felt abandoned and completely alone. It seemed that God himself was gone. Keep in mind that Christ knew the facts, from beginning to end. He was aware of the plan, he willingly participated in human suffering, yet when it came to its cataclysmic climax, he could not even find his Father in heaven.

These were the harsh realities Christ faced. There was no pretending, no minimizing, and no denial. As you face your own harsh realities, you look up and follow Christ. These are the injustices you must face. These are the bone-jarring experiences that must be acknowledged, and in them I hope you hear the voice of Christ saying, "I understand."

After all that had been done to him, Christ was isolated and misunderstood. His lifeless body was taken down from the cross. His friends and family finally acknowledged him, but their comfort for him came too late. It was over, and no one had done the right thing. He was buried. Everyone thought that it was finished. The end. He was gone forever, with no way to redeem what had been taken.

What do you do when well-intentioned friends and family don't give you the right comfort at the right time? What do you do when they look at what has happened to you and think that too much damage has been done, too much self-sabotage has taken place, too much time, energy, and money has been lost? You follow Christ. He knows how it feels to be failed, isolated, and misunderstood. As you look around at all those people and institutions that failed you, who should have done better, should have known better, should have had more faith in you, you follow Christ. He extends his hand to you and says, "I know. This is the way beyond it."

The thing to recognize about Christ's experiences is not only that he had them but that he also conquered them by continuing on the journey. Remember what is stated in the Apostles' Creed: "The third day he rose from the dead." He experienced abuse. He moved through it. He suffered from it. He was conquered by it, and then he turned and conquered it. You follow Christ beyond what has conquered you to a place where you turn and conquer it. That ability is not found in dead places. His grave was empty. It used to be full of death and sorrow, but something powerful, mystical, and miraculous took place. He didn't get stuck there. You don't have to either. The thing about Christ is that he still sends messengers to roll the stone away, to shine light into those crypts that hold darkness and decay in you, to open a way and then show you how to move beyond it.

There is motion to abuse recovery. It is not a static process. It is mostly a glacier-paced motion of facing truth and harsh realities. It is the gradual, fluid river of celebrating silent and secret victories that sometimes are invisible to the outside observer but profoundly apparent to you—that moment when you view yourself as more than a victim and slowly realize you are valued, cherished, loved, and understood by at least One other. Some of the greatest miracles I've ever experienced can never be fully explained to others: sexual victories that brought me back to a place of dignity; anger management that was so effective, no one shuddered around me; a few pounds lost because I tenderly cared for my own body. These miracles don't happen overnight; they happen over time as you follow a path that becomes clear. As you exchange the lies for truth, darkness for light, hate for love, rigidity for grace, and rage for peace, you remain on the path—the one forged by Christ.

Denial and minimizing are not healing tools because they don't embrace truth. They prevent God from having the opportunity to help you find your way forward. Denial is a cheap substitute for faith, and angst is a cheap substitute for passion. You have suffered. You have been betrayed and hurt. You have been abandoned. You have been failed and you have failed. These are things that must be embraced, but there's more to it or you get stuck there.

When I was a teenager, I was very much an outdoor enthusiast. I spent most of my summers backpacking, camping, swimming, and hiking. The summer I was sixteen, I went on a pack trip in the Rocky Mountain backcountry of Colorado. There were about twelve other girls my age and a few brave camp counselors on this trip, which included pack mules and really bad food. A few days into the trip, we stopped for the night and pitched our tents in a ravine. A hard high-country rain suddenly hit, and soon after, a flash flood washed our campsite away. We were cold, miserable, and suddenly homeless! We made several mistakes that have similar repercussions with abuse recovery. We pitched our tents in the wrong place and then stayed there too long. We should have gone to higher ground in the first place, but above all we should have moved as soon as those dark clouds started to gather.

To face your suffering and embrace the injustices are very important aspects to your recovery, but if you pitch your tent there too long, even more damage will set in. You'll be swept away, and then those who hurt you in the first place will conquer you all over again, causing you to remain their victim forever. You can get washed away by bitterness, chaos, and dysfunction if you permit your abuse to fester too long. If you're not careful, it will take everything from you and leave you with more damage than the original abuse. Of course you're angry (or maybe numb). Of course you're outraged (or maybe invisible). Of course the injustice is beyond comprehension, but if you dwell on it too long, you risk becoming just like those who harmed you. You will mishandle others, mishandle yourself, or do both.

It is time to follow Christ, the One who has gone before you. My husband, Tim, and I love to cross-country ski in the Colorado backcountry. Over the years, I have become a wiser woman and realize there are times I need to follow and not lead. Backcountry snow is deep. It takes an enormous amount of energy to break a trail in that snow. Tim is a very strong, physically fit man. I discovered that if he goes before me and breaks through that snow, the trail is much easier on me. All I have to do is glide behind him in two smooth tracks. I still expend a lot of energy to follow the path, but not nearly as much as if I tried to forge one on my own. This is also true in abuse recovery.

When you follow Christ, you follow One who is stronger, One who knows the way, One who makes the path clear for you. As you do, you will discover that the images of your abuser fade from your heart. You will slowly recognize that the image of Christ is replacing your abuser's in your mind, soul, and body. You will glide behind Christ, a fellow abuse survivor, and move beyond your tormentor's actions and damage. You will release yourself from what was imposed on you and follow Christ into a life beyond abuse.

Jesus said, "I know where I came from and where I am going" (John 8:14). At this one last juncture, your voices are connected and your life experiences are joined. You, an abuse survivor, know where you came from. This is focused backward. As you follow Christ, he promises that he knows where he is going. This is focused forward. How do you move beyond abuse? You follow Christ.

## SELF-REFLECTION OR GROUP DISCUSSION

- In what ways have you used your energy to fight a war that is over?

- Christ faced harsh realities. He faced the failure of people and institutions. He was conquered by the human experience, and then he turned around and conquered it. How can following Christ be a vital part of your abuse recovery?

- When you follow Christ, you follow a path of healing that takes place over time. You find connection and commonality with the experiences of Christ on this journey. How do you think following Christ's path will help you be forward focused in your recovery process?

- In what ways do you see Christ differently after reading this book? How might that affect your abuse recovery?

- What are your ideas, feelings, and plans for recovery after reading this book?

# And Finally

The path Christ took was not for the faint of heart. The path to abuse recovery isn't an easy one either. This book is meant to help you consider Christ, perhaps in ways you've not thought of before. These ideas can become components of a larger process.

Maybe you will want to continue your healing journey by finding a therapist or support group. Take those important steps. I have written other books you might also find useful in your recovery process: *The Uncaged Project: Soul Strategies to Rise Above a Wounded Childhood* and the story of my own journey beyond abuse, *Despising the Shame*. In addition, I have an organization to provide people with the spiritual tools to move beyond abuse, called Committed to Freedom Ministries. We have a website (www.committedtofreedom.org) that is full of information, practical helps, and our calendar of events. We offer seminars and retreats in many locations, which we keep posted on our website, as well as inspirational e-mails and other Internet resources that I hope you will take advantage of.

The measuring stick for abuse recovery includes looking at the life of Christ, revisiting your connection to his experiences, and understanding that his work continues in you, beyond your suffering. There is, indeed, life beyond abuse. Pursue it!

Sallie Culbreth
Committed to Freedom Ministries
PO Box 20916
Hot Springs, Arkansas 71903-0916
1-800-713-7837
www.committedtofreedom.org

# How to Find a Counselor

The word *counselor* is often misused or misunderstood. It is a legal term. It is also a term that is interchangeable with the word *therapist*. This section is, by no means, exhaustive. It is meant to provide you with a simple framework of understanding and resources available to those who seek counseling. Use it as a springboard to finding the appropriate direction for your circumstances.

There are many factors to consider when searching for help with your abuse issues. The first consideration is who to go to. Do you go to a pastor? A friend? A therapist? To make a wise decision, you have to do your homework. There is no guarantee an individual who is a member of the clergy or a licensed therapist is necessarily the right person for you and your recovery process. A good beginning place is through word of mouth. Do you have friends or family members who have successfully worked with a counselor? Listen and ask questions. This can give you a great deal of insight into who to go to and where to start.

There are many things to consider before you take this important step. Many pastors are wise and have great people-helping skills but may lack the knowledge or skills to help you wade through the debris of sexual abuse. Therapists, too, have varying degrees of training and effectiveness of treatment plans that you should be aware of. You are about to invest a great deal of time and money if you pursue counseling, and you want to make certain you make an appropriate choice.

First, you must decide what kind of help you want. There are several categories of helpers you need to be aware of as you make this decision.

## Friends and Family

Those you trust the most may be a valuable source of support and encouragement. There are many people gifted with wisdom, compassion, and sensitivity. These will be important relationships for you as you journey toward abuse recovery.

## Clergy

Pastors and pastoral staff are people who can provide you with a theological and spiritual perspective on some of your issues concerning God and abuse recovery. Use caution, as you would with anyone, to carefully weigh the spiritual insights and practices that may be helpful. Often clergy are so overwhelmed with other responsibilities that they might not be able to dedicate the time you need to weather the long process of abuse recovery. They may also not have the awareness of abuse issues that is necessary to help survivors work through damage in a thorough way. Some pastors may have a resource list of counselors they know have good reputations, but you will still need to do your homework and decide which one is the right counselor for you.

## Pastoral Counselors

Pastoral counselors use both spirituality and psychotherapy. They are most often ministers who combine religious resources with psychology. Pastoral counselors are certified mental health counselors who also have extensive theological training.

## Mental Health Counselors

In order to practice mental health counseling, helping professionals must first invest a significant number of years to academic training and supervision and then become licensed and certified. They follow a strict code of ethics that must be maintained in order to remain licensed. You can verify a counselor's credentials by checking with your state's professional counselor licensure board. In general, mental health counselors are not able to prescribe medications, such as antidepressants.

Therapists practice different forms of counseling, and you should be familiar with what types yours uses before you consent to become his or her client. The theoretical framework that a therapist works from might be great for someone else and not at all helpful to you. There are many models used in therapy. The following list covers a generalization of the major models therapists use:

- *Psychodynamic*—these models (such as Freud's psychoanalytic therapy or Adlerian therapy) emphasize insight into deeply buried problems.
- *Relationship-Oriented*—these models (such as existential, person-centered, or Gestalt) emphasize emotional exploration and subjective experiences centered on the therapist-client relationship as the catalyst for healing.
- *Cognitive Behavioral*—these models (such as cognitive therapy, rational emotive behavior therapy, or solution-focused brief therapy) address disruptive thinking patterns through structure, psychoeducation, and homework.
- *Family*—these models (such as family systems therapy or marriage therapy) work with an entire system, of which an individual is a part, as a way to better understand the individuals in that system. Therapists who work with any of the other three models may also work with family systems.

You and the therapist need to go through an interview process to make certain both of you are comfortable with each other. Good counselors will provide you with a process called "informed consent" during the initial session. This is usually some form of written statement as well as verbal information sharing. Informed consent means you understand the counselor's fees, schedules, objectives, and treatment plan. If you will use insurance to pay for your sessions, you must clearly understand how that will work, how reimbursement occurs, and how many sessions your insurance will pay for. If you are part of a managed-care program, there will most likely be a very limited number of sessions you are allowed to have (sometimes as few as six). This is all part of the process of making a decision regarding which counselor to choose.

Valid questions to ask a counselor include his education, certification, and licensing; how long he has been in practice; what his treatment model is and why he thinks it will work for you; what his expectations are for the outcome of your therapy; what expenses will most likely be involved in your therapy (not just fees but books, retreat or seminar fees, and other resources that might be prescribed during your treatment); and how he will address cultural and value differences that are significant to you.

## PSYCHIATRISTS

Psychiatrists are medical doctors who have specialized in psychiatry. They often work in conjunction with family doctors and therapists to provide treatment to clients who need their level of help. Because they are physicians, they can prescribe medications, conduct diagnostic tests, and practice therapy. They must be certified through the American Board of Psychiatry and Neurology and have an unrestricted license to practice medicine in the United States.

## SUPPORT GROUPS

The group experience is often helpful in the abuse recovery process. Many churches and community centers offer support groups conducted by minimally trained facilitators. Some support groups use a book or workbook as their discussion focus. Others adhere to a less structured, nondirective format. These groups offer a much-needed sense of community, understanding, and support that can greatly contribute to your journey of healing. There are also therapeutic groups available that are conducted by a trained mental health professional. These groups have a more therapy-focused purpose, but support, understanding, and encouragement are also experienced by many abuse survivors.

Support groups are not for everyone. Confidentiality cannot be completely assured in a group because the members are not legally bound to protect fellow members. This is an important thing to remember as you determine whether or not to participate in a group. Be certain you have a clear understanding of what the group does, who will conduct the group, how long the group will meet, if there are fees involved and how those fees will be paid, whether the group is open or closed (meaning that once the group begins, no one else may join), and if you are free to leave the group at any time should you choose to.

## RESOURCE INFORMATION TO FIND LICENSED HELPING PROFESSIONALS

To move beyond abuse will involve all of who you are — body, mind, and spirit. God placed himself in the midst of your life so that you would be connected to him, enlightened, and strengthened for the journey. God has also placed dedicated, trained, and compassionate people all around you. They can help navigate you through some of the stickier stages of abuse recovery.

The following are just a few organizations that will help you locate an appropriate counselor for your needs and circumstances:

**American Association of Christian Counselors** (www.aacc.net)
PO Box 739
Forest, VA 24551
Phone: 800-526-8673
Fax: 434-525-9480

**American Association of Pastoral Counselors** (www.aapc.org)
9504A Lee Highway
Fairfax, VA 22031-2303
Phone: 703-385-6967
Fax: 703-352-7725

**American Board of Psychiatry and Neurology, Inc.**
(www.abpn.com)
2150 E. Lake Cook Road, Suite 900
Buffalo Grove, IL 60089
Phone: 847-229-6500
Fax: 847-229-6600

**American Mental Health Counselors Association**
(www.amhca.org)
801 N. Fairfax Street Suite 304
Alexandria, VA 22314
Phone: 800-326-2642
Fax: 703-548-4775

**National Board for Certified Counselors** (www.nbcc.org)
3 Terrace Way
Greensboro, NC 27403-3660
Phone: 336-547-0607
Fax: 336-547-0017

# Author

SALLIE CULBRETH is the founder of Committed to Freedom Ministries, which offers Christian recovery resources for survivors of childhood abuse. She holds a bachelor's degree in pastoral ministries and a master's degree in counseling studies.

# More resources from NavPress!

### The Wounded Heart
Dr. Dan B. Allender
978-1-60006-307-7

Now repackaged, but with the same life-giving insights, *The Wounded Heart* will help survivors and their loved ones find professional skill and spiritual direction to learn that they can heal from the trauma of abuse.

### The Wounded Heart Workbook
Dr. Dan B. Allender with Karen Lee-Thorp
978-1-60006-308-4

Don't forget *The Wounded Heart Workbook*, designed to be used alone or in a group. With special sections for men and group discussions, survivors can take specific steps to work through the pain of abuse.

### Helping Those Who Hurt
Barbara M. Roberts
978-1-60006-382-4

This step-by-step handbook guides readers through grief, death, troubled marriages, suicide, and other life crises with wisdom from the author's firsthand experience. Personal vignettes, lists, and how-to's make it an ideal resource for those who are hurting as well as for those ministering to the hurt person.

To order copies, call NavPress at 1-800-366-7788
or log on to www.navpress.com.

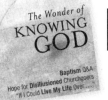

Here's a resource
to help you pray
with more

# Power,
## *Passion,*
# & Purpose

---

### Every issue of *Pray!* brings you:

- **Special Themes** that deal with specific, often groundbreaking topics of interest that will help you grow in your passion and effectiveness in prayer
- **Features** on important and intriguing aspects of prayer, both personal and corporate
- **Ideas** to stimulate creativity in your prayer life and in the prayer life of your church
- **Empowered**, a special section written by church prayer leaders, for church prayer leaders
- **Prayer News** from around the world, to get you up-to-date with what God is doing through prayer all over the globe
- **Prayer Journeys**, a guest-authored column sharing how God moved him or her closer to Jesus through prayer
- **Intercession Ignited**, providing encouragement, inspiration, and insight for people called to the ministry of intercession
- **Classics**, featuring time-tested writings about prayer from men and women of God through the centuries
- **Inspiring Art** from a publication that has been recognized nationally for its innovative approach to design
- And much, much more!

---

No Christian who wants to connect more deeply with God
should be without *Pray!*

## Six issues of *Pray!* are only $21.97*

Canadian and international subscriptions are only $27.97 (Includes Canadian GST).

*plus sales tax where applicable